Growing Young

Growing Young

Embracing the Joy and Accepting the Challenges of Mid-Life

Lois Mowday Rabey

WATERBROOK
PRESS

GROWING YOUNG
PUBLISHED BY WATERBROOK PRESS
5446 North Academy Boulevard, Suite 200
Colorado Springs, Colorado 80918
A division of Random House, Inc.

All stories told in this book have been used with permission. Details in some
anecdotes and stories have been changed to protect the identities of the persons
involved.

ISBN 1-57856-143-4

Published in association with the literary agency of
Alive Communications, Inc.
1465 Kelly Johnson Blvd., Suite 320
Colorado Springs, Colorado 80920

Printed in the United States of America
1999—First Edition

10 9 8 7 6 5 4 3 2 1

Contents

Introduction: Celebrating Change vii

1   Embracing New Ideals   1

2   Discovering Your Inner Beauty 15

3   Cultivating Healthy Habits 27

4   Taking Control of Your Journey
    Through Menopause 43

5   Enjoying All the Phases of Motherhood 57

6   Welcoming the Changing Seasons of Marriage 71

7   Appreciating Your Sexuality 85

8   Making the Most of Singleness 97

9   Grandmothering with Joy   113

10 Caring for Your Aging Parents 127

11 Cherishing Your Friendships 139

12 Resting in the Promise of Immortality 149

13 Savoring Your Yesterdays 159

14 Rediscovering God 167

Conclusion: Growing Young 177

Celebrating ✳ Change

I 'VE ALWAYS SEEN MYSELF as a planner, an anticipator, a woman prepared for what lies ahead. Never caught in the rain without an umbrella or away from home without emergency cash, most days I'm ready for whatever comes. My ever-present Day-Timer outlines my to-do list, which I generally get done.

Well, that's how I USED to operate.

Then I turned forty-four. Within a thirteen-month period, a number of life-changing events occurred: I remarried after ten years of widowhood, my youngest daughter graduated from high school and went off to college, my mother died, my eldest daughter married, and menopausal symptoms descended with drenching force.

I was so surprised. I still am.

Change became the norm instead of the exception. Some of these changes were painful, and ALL were different from previous changes I'd experienced. I'd anticipated moving through midlife the way I had moved through other life stages: taking things in stride, letting go and looking forward to the future, defying the aging process, and overcoming painful times with determination and faith. Instead I found myself mourning losses, battling fear about the future, feeling betrayed by my body, and questioning long-held beliefs.

For the past decade I have been trying to adjust to the strangeness of myself. When I was in my twenties and thirties, I never thought I would become my own source of anxiety. I had always believed I would have plenty of time to correct any incongruities in my life, to improve relationships, to whip myself into better physical shape, to finish tomorrow what I had failed to accomplish today.

But with the advent of midlife, I found myself sliding down the other side of life's proverbial hill with the black crepe-paper streamers flowing behind me. From my appearance to my spirituality, every part of me was undergoing a metamorphosis. Thankfully the downslide of "middlescence" moderated into a pleasant pace, and surprises became less shocking and more manageable. In time, I changed my thinking and adjusted my attitude.

I now DAILY live by the verse, "Do not conform any longer to the pattern of this world, but be transformed by the renewing of your mind" (Romans 12:2). This world views the process of aging as an enemy, but God gives wisdom, opportunity, and freshness to those who are in relationship with him:

The righteous will flourish like a palm tree,
    they will grow like a cedar of Lebanon;
planted in the house of the LORD,
    they will flourish in the courts of our God.
They will still bear fruit in old age,
    they will stay fresh and green,
proclaiming, "The LORD is upright;
    he is my Rock, and there is no wickedness in him."
                                        (PSALM 92:12-15)

Part of being able to flourish as God intended is to think differently about aging. Instead of succumbing to our culture's view, we can infuse our spirits with God's view. We have to make a choice. We have to decide how we will respond to this transforming time of life. Will we view the rest of our life as a strenuous attempt to survive as long as we can, or will we embrace a fresh perspective on what lies ahead? Will we wither away or "bear fruit" and "stay fresh and green"?

"Growing young" is not just a play on words to trick our minds into believing a frothy half-truth. It is a phrase that enlarges our perspective on growing old to include some long-abandoned attributes of youth. In a manner reminiscent of our childhood days, many of us find ourselves freed from some responsibilities of adulthood as we move through midlife. We now reap the benefits of wisdom gained from life experiences, freedom to be ourselves in new ways, excitement at the prospect of learning more, and joy in giving to others from the wealth of our own story. We can live richly, drawing on the wisdom of age and the abandon of youth. It is exciting!

This book highlights some of the joys and challenges you will likely encounter during these transition years. Most of the stories within these pages come from my experience, but I also write about the experiences of other women. Some may evoke a chuckle, others a tear. All are intended to resonate with you and help you enjoy your journey. My prayer is that you will be able to celebrate who you are at this God-ordained stage of your life and that you will find the motivation and courage to continue to flourish as you grow young.

Embracing
New ❖ Ideals

A HILL RISES above the landscape of America. I don't know if similar hills dot the horizons of other countries, but this one looms large in the United States. It symbolizes our progression through life from birth to death. We are born at the bottom of the hill, looking up toward the summit of early midlife. Most of us move toward the apex with energy and determination. Up, up, up we go. We're part of this nation's ideal: young, strong, beautiful, healthy, successful, and enjoying a quality of life unsurpassed anywhere on earth.

As we near the pinnacle, we anticipate what it will be like to have arrived. To have scaled the challenges of young adulthood, reared our families, secured our careers, and finally earned the right to bask in the enjoyment of tasks well done.

But as soon as we catch our breath after our arduous climb to the top, we find ourselves sliding down the shadowed slope of middle age. Our youth is gone. As we look in the mirror, we see the faces of our mothers. Friends, decked out in black, give us parties that resemble funerals, complete with gifts of medicinal ointments for ailments foreign to the young.

Many of us attempt to climb back toward the other side of the hill. Most find it difficult to accept the inevitable: We are aging. It doesn't help that we live in a youth-obsessed culture. Attitudes about aging have long been reflected in our advertising, television programming, and cultural values. We give lip service to growing old gracefully, but we deny that aging will ever happen to us. Ironically, we want to live long, long lives, but we don't accept the truth about what that means. We cling to the illusion that we can be fifty, sixty, seventy, even eighty, and not look any older than we did at thirty or forty!

According to the Bible, age brings wisdom and understanding (Job 12:12), older people should be treated with respect (Leviticus 19:32), and older women are to teach younger women (Titus 2:4). But these practices rarely prevail today. As Christians, we are called to follow biblical teaching and not succumb to the ways of the world, but we are influenced by the attitudes of the day.

It doesn't have to be this way. We can view this stage of life as a time to acknowledge how far we have come and all we have learned along the way. We can change our own attitudes toward aging. For instance, the next time you throw a birthday party for a friend who turns forty or fifty, you can choose to pass by the rows of black party items. Rather than giving her a premature wake, treat her to a party that affirms life.

When my good friend Susan turned fifty, she requested just such an event. Twenty of her closest female friends gathered at my house, which was filled with fresh flowers and brightly colored balloons. Each woman brought her favorite casserole, and we feasted around a crystal- and china-laden table. Candles and dim lights wrapped our festive dinner in the warm glow of friendship and gratitude.

After dinner Susan gave each woman a gift and told the group about the unique and precious relationship she shared with each friend. All the gifts we gave to her were lovely presents we knew she'd love. There wasn't a black item in the bunch! The evening was a wonderful expression of mutual love and respect.

If a stranger had been peeking through the window, she would have concluded that our attitude about aging was one of appreciation for the goodness of life at the halfway mark.

Now that's something to celebrate. And celebrate we did!

On my way to speak at a conference in Palm Springs,
I stopped at an outlet mall.
I felt pretty good until a sales clerk offered
me an additional 15 percent discount on a purchase.
"Why?" I asked.
She pointed to a sign by the cash register that read,
Tuesday is senior discount day!
I was not even fifty yet,
and the qualifying age was fifty-five.

※❖※

The people who ask women
who are not pregnant
when their babies are due
also operate cash registers
at stores offering senior discounts.
They don't mean to hurt you.
Laugh and eat chocolate.

A recent newspaper article profiled
a well-known businesswoman.
The article included information about
her grown children
DECLINED
and her marriage of thirty-some years.
But when the journalist inquired about
the woman's age,
she declined to give an answer.

✧✦✧

TRUTH
Refusing to tell your age reinforces an
attitude of shame.
The facts of our lives usually reveal the
truth anyway.
Better to answer honestly and with a smile.

ANSWER HONESTLY

My first husband, Jack, and I met in high school.
One day while sitting on the beach, I noticed him staring at me.
"What are you thinking?" I asked.
"I was picturing you at age fifty
and wondering what you'd look like."
I imagined that I would need to be youthful looking
in order to meet with his approval and satisfy him as a wife.
I did marry him, but our dreams of growing old together were
shattered when he was killed in a hot-air-balloon accident.
I've gone on through midlife without Jack, I've turned fifty,
and I've put aside the image I thought I'd have to maintain
in order to keep my husband happy.

❧

Our youthful expectations affect our attitudes in maturity.
As a young adult you held in your mind an image
of what you'd look and act like
as a woman in midlife.
That picture was distorted.
Let go of it.

When I was a child,
I talked like a child,
I thought like a child,
I reasoned like a child.

When I became a [woman],
I put childish ways behind me.

1 CORINTHIANS 13:11

It's becoming easier to watch some
of the women on television
and in the movies.
Middle-aged actresses such as
Candace Bergen, Mary Tyler Moore,
Meryl Streep, Diane Keaton,
Barbra Streisand, and Sally Field
are beginning to change the celluloid
image of women.

Public attitudes are beginning to
shift with the changing demographics.
Take heart.

When Rebecca turned forty,
she celebrated for two-and-a-half months.
Parties and special dinners with
friends and family lasted from
early September through   PERSPECTIVE
Thanksgiving.

⚞❖❟

A healthy attitude
results in celebration.
If you are dreading your next birthday,
ask God to help change your perspective.
Remember, your view of yourself
affects how others see you.

HEALTHY ATTITUDE

The movie *Titanic* is told from the
viewpoint of elderly Rose, who is reminiscing about her
survival of the sinking ship.
An eighty-seven-year-old actress
plays the one-hundred-and-one-year-old character.
Her audience is her granddaughter
and a team of explorers
combing the wreckage of the *Titanic*
for lost treasure.
That audience and the one in the theater
spend over three hours entranced by
this weathered character as she tells her story.
Even with wrinkled face and
gnarled hands, she holds our attention
with a lovely grace.

⚜

The older we are,
the more unforgettable events
and breathless moments
we've experienced.
We can help those younger than ourselves
look toward aging
with anticipation instead of dread
as we spin our yarns for them.
Tell your stories.

"I always did what was expected," Ann mused.
"I've always expected that a woman my age
would be mellow.
But now that I'm forty-five,
I don't want a leisurely lifestyle.
I want to stay active and start new things.
I guess I need to be willing to change my
attitude about how a woman my age
should act."

Many of us have been taught not to rock the boat,
even our own.
Give up conformity for conformity's sake,
and look for ways to express
the real you.

Conformity is one of the most
fundamental dishonesties of all.

When we reject our specialness,
water down our God-given
individuality and uniqueness, we
begin to lose our freedom.

The conformist is in no way a free man.
He has to follow the herd.

NORMAN VINCENT PEALE
Man, Morals and Maturity

I was checking in at an airline ticket counter
when I noticed a man to my right staring at me
　　　with appreciation.
I smiled to myself and felt a wonderful
　　　surge of self-assurance.
Then I caught a glimpse of a young woman
on my left who was smiling past me
　　　at the man.
APPRECIATION
My admirer wasn't my admirer after all.
I suddenly resented him and felt
anger toward the young woman.

Our momentary disappointments
can turn our attitudes against us,
ruining a perfectly fine day.
Remind yourself that you are more than
how you look to others.
Keep smiling internally and accept yourself
exactly as you are.
ACCEPT YOURSELF

I adored my grandmother.
If I had been asked when I was a child
who I wanted to be when I grew up,
I would have said I wanted to grow up
to be just like her.

Children often look at older people with
love and admiration.
Perhaps we should recapture some of our
childlike wonderment
toward seasoned adults.

Our church has a youthful congregation.
For years I've been one of the few members
with white hair.
Recently some midlifers-and-older
have joined our ranks.
When I'm with women older than I am,
I feel comfort and a desire to ask them
about all aspects of life.

❧

We forget that age really does bring
increased wisdom.
Learn from those older than yourself,
and keep teaching those younger.

Is not wisdom found
among the aged?
Does not long life
bring understanding?

JOB 12:12

Discoveríng ✢ Your
Inner ✢ Beauty

B EAUTY IS ONLY SKIN DEEP. It's what is beneath the surface that matters.

Well...yes, kind of. In theory and theology, it's true that what's
inside is far more important than how we look on the outside.
Most of us believe that God's definition of beauty is the one we
should embrace. He tells us that our concern should be for our
inner spirit rather than outward adornment (1 Peter 3:3-4).

But because the media inundate us with images of visual per-
fection, we are subject to the delusion that we must—and can—look
eternally youthful. What the beauty industry doesn't tell us is how
soft-focus camera lenses and cosmetic surgery distort our percep-
tion of aging. Those in the beauty business present the illusion that
it's possible for any woman to keep her youthful looks. And we
want to believe them.

We all know that, while external beauty may not reflect our true
worth as women, beautiful people certainly capture our attention.
Pretty girls and women are the ones most photographed for

advertisements, and they pull in astronomical sums of money to grace the covers of magazines. We learn from an early age that a lovely appearance and popularity often go hand in hand; the most attractive girls are usually the first ones asked to school parties or out on dates.

During midlife, however, the internal physiological changes that occur ultimately defy our attempts to camouflage our appearance. What a face-lift may hide, age-spotted hands expose. I never intended to show dramatic signs of aging (with the exception of my prematurely white hair in high school—obviously, not a sign of age for me!). I told myself that I would NOT gain weight, would NOT let my wrinkles show, would NOT succumb to fashion that put comfort above style. I would defy the aging process with grace.

Phooey! It didn't work. I dislike pain too much to go under the knife for cosmetic surgery. Even the most expensive makeup doesn't conceal the telltale signs of days in the sun and years on the calendar. A Crisco-coated ten pounds refuses to burn off, and I wear slacks with elastic in the waist. In the past, I would have considered that just too old-ladyish. Now I gladly enjoy the comfort of eating a meal and breathing at the same time!

As my appearance has changed, so has my perspective on getting older. Most women I know who are over forty-five also have learned to accept themselves as they are. We can easily spot a woman who hasn't accepted her age and actually grieve a little for her. How uncomfortable she must be in her too-tight skirt and super-high heels.

There's no need to look dowdy, and we have plenty of reasons to work hard at taking care of our bodies. But let's not try to look like we're still in our twenties.

Changes in our appearance are the most obvious signs of midlife, and these changes will be easier to accept if we are honest about them and open to changing our minds about what is beautiful. As we rethink our values, we will begin to appreciate our internal beauty as women created in the image of God.

I look in the mirror and I am shocked.
I still struggle with feelings
        of disgust and disappointment.
I feel guilty for placing a high value on
        physical attractiveness,
but the compliments I receive these days
are rarely more encouraging than
"Gee, you look good…for your age."
That's nice, but it just reinforces the truth
that I look good only compared to
negative stereotypes of older women.
This issue is, for me, one of the most difficult
        to reconcile
as I continue to display the visible signs
        of aging.
I'm making progress, but it's tough.

❧✦❧

While God values inner beauty over
        external beauty,
many of us still place a high priority on
        having a youthful appearance.
Be honest with yourself about your values,
and work hard on changing your mind about
        what's realistic and important.

My mail-ordered package of super-luxurious hand lotion
arrived in a box too large to contain just one bottle.
Nestled among the Styrofoam peanuts was, indeed,
another item. I eagerly opened a vinyl cosmetic bag
bulging with as-yet-unknown treasures.
Fifteen—count 'em— fifteen miniature tubes and vials
of youth-promising elixirs spilled out onto my kitchen table.
There was uniquely formulated help for my eyelids, eye
corners, lips, chin, hands, thighs, feet, and elbows.
I dabbed several samples on the back of my hand,
then panicked. What happens when you put eye cream on
your thigh or chin lotion on your feet or, in my case, the
whole mess on your hands?
I thought fleetingly about ordering the thigh cream
that promised to obliterate cellulite.
Then I tossed the cosmetic bag and its contents into the trash
and enjoyed my one original purchase.

Advertisers try to convince us that we can alter
our appearance to recapture the dewy beauty of youth.
Age changes our physical appearance.
Accept that fact.

> Charm is deceptive,
> and beauty is fleeting.
>
> PROVERBS 31:30

"She looks pretty good,"
my husband, Steve, said to me
after meeting a woman he knew to be over fifty.
"She's had a lift," I replied, somewhat arrogantly.
He looked surprised and asked me how I knew.
I informed him that you can usually tell
by the unnatural-looking result of cosmetic surgery.
Taut skin doesn't stretch smoothly over
a face that is fifty years old.
While I haven't tried surgery,
I've tested numerous brands of moisturizers
with the hope that my wrinkles really will disappear
and I'll look years younger than I am.
Instead I just look overly made up.

❧❖❧

Attempts to camouflage our age
are usually detectable.
Be careful not to fool yourself.
Make an honest evaluation before
investing dollars in products and procedures
that may not get you what you really want.

Marta had relished the compliments
that frequently came her way as a young woman.
By the time she was forty-five,
she had become weary with the struggle
to hold on to a physical beauty that was
fading with age.
She cast away all restraint and told herself she no
longer cared about how she looked.
She stopped wearing makeup and started
eating compulsively.

❧❦❧

While emphasis on physical appearance,
especially unrealistic attempts to look
        younger than we are,
is worth giving up,
total disregard for our appearance is wrong too.
Complementing our natural beauty
with moderate makeup, a healthy diet,
regular exercise, and stylish clothing
        appropriate for our age
enhances our sense of well-being.
Give up the extremes and adopt
a reasonable regimen of personal physical care.

We were out to dinner with friends
when we ran into Janet and her husband.
We spoke briefly and then took our own seats.
Our friends commented on Janet's beauty.
While her physical appearance testifies to
          her midlife age,
her countenance and manner
are alluring and magnetic.
People are drawn to Janet
and often describe her in terms
          usually reserved
for depictions of physical beauty.
Janet has accepted herself, her age,
and her worth in God's eyes.

When a woman has achieved
          internal peace,
she manifests it in her appearance.
She has a look of well-being
          and contentment
that transcends the physical beauty
that fades with age.
Look inside yourself and to God
for an awareness of
          beauty that lasts.

Your beauty should not come from outward adornment, such as braided hair and the wearing of gold jewelry and fine clothes.

Instead, it should be that of your inner self, the unfading beauty of a gentle and quiet spirit, which is of great worth in God's sight.

1 PETER 3:3-4

Six of us were engrossed in girl talk
at a crowded, popular dinner spot.
Five of the six of us were in our
forties and fifties.
We were animated, laughing,
and listening to each other
as the conversation bounced around the table.
The waitress told us that several customers
had commented on the table with
the "great-looking women."
We were surprised and pleased.
Only one of us still had the bloom of youth,
yet others saw beauty in all of us
as we interacted.

❧❖❧

Our souls live forever,
long after outer beauty fades.
Enjoy the depth of each other's soul.

A thing of beauty is a joy forever:

Its loveliness increases; it will never

pass into nothingness.

JOHN KEATS
Endymion

My daughter and her husband gave me a frame
to go around my car license plate that read,
"I'd rather be shopping at Nordstroms."
I received it in the fun spirit that it was given
and put it on my car.
Some people probably judge me harshly
because of it.
That's okay. I'm kind of asking for it.
I also know that I used to be
very quick to judge by appearances.
I concluded that women
who didn't dress with style
were probably not too savvy.
Now I know better.
Savvy about fashion? Perhaps not.
Wonderful women? Almost always.
Impressions can be deceiving.

Such is beauty ever—
neither here nor there,
now nor then—neither
in Rome nor in Athens,
but wherever there is a
soul to admire.

THOREAU

As we age, we begin to grasp that it takes
time, knowledge, and understanding
to uncover beauty in ourselves and in others.
Become a soul searcher.

The other day I bought some foundation.
I walked around the various cosmetic islands
in a local department store
and read all the results promised with each product.
Then I went to the drugstore
and bought, for one-third the price,
a brand my mother used.
I feel better.

It's normal to want to look young.
The danger lies in chasing after false idols.
Grieve the loss of one kind of beauty
and move on to receive another.

The women I admire most are givers.
My respect for them has absolutely nothing
to do with outward appearance.
But the beauty they display
by their attitudes and actions
touches my soul.
They embrace the values of their Creator.
They are close to God.

What God values
touches others
with love.
Cultivate your relationship with God.

Man looks at the outward appearance,
but the Lord looks at the heart.

1 SAMUEL 16:7

Cultivating

Healthy ❖ Habits

GOD CREATED US as physical and spiritual beings. His Holy Spirit lives in us. We are to care for our bodies as the temple of this Spirit (1 Corinthians 6:19).

The midlife years bring changes in our bodies, requiring that we adjust our lifestyles to maintain our health and physical well-being. With the onset of middlescence comes a concern for disease prevention and health maintenance. No longer can we eat whatever we like. We begin to think about exercising to maintain our health, not just for weight management. This attention to health is part of being good stewards of the bodies God has given us.

Even though I've been in the middle zone for years, I'm always surprised when my generally good health gets disrupted. The aches and pains are often small and no more than bothersome, but I didn't used to hurt at all. Recently my daughter Lisa and I gave a baby shower for my younger daughter, Lara. The day of the shower I ran around town picking up the cake, snacks, party goodies, and flowers. When I got home, I cleaned the main level of our house and placed extra chairs in the family room. Thirty energetic women filled that room for several hours that night as Lara reveled in the attention and love that was poured out on her and her yet-to-be-born baby.

After everyone left, I collapsed on the couch. My feet hurt, and I was exhausted. The next day I just couldn't get moving and was amazed at my level of fatigue. I have never had trouble with aching feet until this year. My energy level is high most of the time, and I usually bounce back from a day of heavy activity by the next morning.

It is difficult to admit that my body is showing signs of being around for fifty-two years. Other women my age tell me they feel the same way. Even those of us in the best of health notice changes that we can't attribute to anything other than advancing age. But a wonderful quality of life is still well within the grasp of most of us if we are aware of these inevitable changes and make an effort to cultivate healthy habits.

Once I realized my health
would be affected by my age,
I started to imagine
all manner of illnesses
headed my way.
At first I didn't go for the
recommended yearly physical.
I was afraid.

Many, many women enjoy good health
well into their much-later years.
Don't assume your health will
dramatically decline.

Who of you by worrying
can add a single hour to his life?

MATTHEW 6:27

I didn't get my first routine,
preventive physical until I was fifty-one.
I found a woman internist
and had a lengthy conversation with her nurse.
I told her I was unaware of anything
wrong with me, but I wanted
a complete physical that would tell me exactly
how I was doing for a woman my age.
I had blood work done, all the usual
pressure-taking and ear-poking.
I even held my breath and had the
never-mentioned exam for colon cancer—
do you know what I mean?
It didn't hurt and was more
palatable to receive from a woman doctor.
I felt old,
submitting to so much evaluation.
But the results were better than I
would ever have imagined.
Low cholesterol and many other good reports.

❧

Not all health news is bad.
It's encouraging to know exactly what is
happening in your body.
Schedule a full, preventive physical.
Repeat it routinely.

I felt the first of many breast lumps
when I was in my early forties.

DISCOVERY

It is difficult not to jump to frightening conclusions
at the thought of breast cancer.
Within two days of my discovery,
I had seen my doctor,
had a mammogram,
and been diagnosed cancer-free.

～❖～

Breast cancer is a real health issue for
midlife women. MAMMOGRAM
Call your doctor at the first sign of a lump,
get a mammogram as soon as your
doctor recommends,
and support the many women who are facing the
challenges of this disease.

CHALLENGES

The other day I saw a new
magazine on the rack.
Its title told me nothing,
but its table of contents—
articles about health and
attitude and the usual fashion bits—
revealed that it's geared to midlife women.
I already subscribe to a health magazine and
regularly buy other publications that catch my eye.
Sometimes my kids tease me about this
"mature woman" reading material.
I just smile and read on.

✿

Information leads to prevention.
Start educating yourself.

My membership card at the local
health club dates back to 1990.
Every year I think about dropping my
membership because of the sporadic way
I work out.
I go for a few months.
I quit.
I go again.
I quit again.
I've also purchased workout
videos to use at home.
They bore me.
Finally I purchased an inexpensive treadmill,
and now I work out while watching the *Today* show.
I don't get bored, and I exercise more often.
The days I work out, I feel much
better than the days I don't.

❧❖❧

Everything I have ever read about health care
states that exercise is good for you.
It's never too late to start moving.

Most of the midlife women I know
have given up on dieting.
They admit that diets don't work;
they are difficult to follow and
generally don't produce lasting results.
One of my friends has lost weight
by grocery shopping every few days
and buying fresh fruits and vegetables
in small quantities.
She used to buy large quantities,
and the items would spoil before
she could eat them,
so she'd grab a handful of cookies instead.
Now she has delicious, healthy food on hand
when she's hungry.
She's slowly lost fifteen pounds and is
on her way to a permanent lifestyle change.

We are more likely to maintain good health
when our weight is
within the recommended range—
a range that is often less than what we
currently weigh.
Don't give up.
Keep trying to eat in healthier ways.
Eating well prolongs life and improves its quality.

I've been on a constant diet for the last
two decades. I've lost a total of 789 pounds.

By all accounts, I should be hanging from
a charm bracelet.

ERMA BOMBECK

Every year I visit my friend Claudette in Florida.
We walk to the beach in the morning,
go shopping, eat lunch at a waterside café,
and head back to her house by midafternoon.
Then Claudette naps.
I don't nap when I'm home,
but I do when I'm with her.
Her guest room has shutters and a ceiling fan.
I close out the bright sun, turn the fan on low,
and doze.
We never rest for more than an hour,
and usually it's for only about twenty minutes.
It's a wonderful break.
I think I'll add it to my at-home routine.

A little rest can revive you for hours.
Try it.
If you work in an office,
close your door and stretch out on the floor.
If you don't have a door,
try a ten-minute rest time in your car after lunch.
If none of those options work,
take the first fifteen minutes at home after work
just to sit with your feet up
and enjoy a few moments of stillness.

Marcia is a good friend and also
a wonderful massage therapist.

MASSAGE

As she works her magic on my
aching muscles, we talk about our lives.
Until recently Marcia was a nutritional devotee.
She would cringe at the very mention of my
favorite elixir—coffee.
No chemical ever passed her lips.
I saw her last week, and she was transformed.
She told me of her decision to embrace a more
moderate approach to her health care.

MODERATION

She spoke fondly of chocolate and the desire to
enjoy in moderation some once-forbidden goodies.
I applauded her newfound philosophy.

✦✦✦

Our culture is so obsessed with avoiding death
that sometimes life is reduced to a
prescribed list of restrictions and regimens.
Accept your mortality.
Give up compulsive health care
and choose moderation.

MORTALITY

I am such a worrier.
At the first sign of ill health,
I pull down my massive
Mayo Clinic Health Guide
to diagnose my illness
and gather treatment suggestions.
My book is a little more worn
now that I'm in midlife.
With each read, I determine to
eat better, exercise more,
and see my doctor annually.
My list of preventive measures grows.
It's burdensome.

Midlife health issues can cause us
to worry and struggle to our ill
instead of to our good.
Be sensible, do what you can,
and relax.

Preserving the health
by too severe
a rule is a
wearisome malady.
LA ROCHEFOUCAULD

At least once a month, Monte and Linda
come over for dinner.
We all love beef
but have cut it out of our diets—
            most of the time—
for health reasons.
At our monthly dinners, however,
we splurge.
Filets with hollandaise sauce,
roast beef with roasted potatoes,
T-bone steaks with baked potatoes
smothered in butter and sour cream!
We feast to our hearts' content.

＞◈＜

Practicing healthy habits doesn't mean you
give up all your favorite delicacies all the time.
Plan a lovely dinner and indulge.

When I'm exercising in the morning
and watching the *Today* show,
I often catch the segment in which
Willard Scott wishes "Happy Birthday"
to people 100 years old or more.
I think that's a nice thing to do.
Then I see article after article
in magazines and newspapers
about the quest to prolong life.
Sometimes I think we try to kid ourselves
into thinking that our bodies will last forever—
if we can just hang on until science finds
cures for every disease imaginable.

Our bodies do not live forever.
Be thankful that our souls do.

For God so loved the world that
he gave his one and only Son, that
whoever believes in him shall not
perish but have eternal life.

JOHN 3:16

MORE · HEALTHY · HABITS

⊛ Consider which vitamins and other dietary supplements might be helpful to you. Most people in health food stores can assist you in deciding what to buy. Consult your doctor to make sure you aren't overdoing supplements.

⊛ While we often assume that most women no longer smoke, many do. If you do, try again and again to stop. Smoking is one of the most harmful contributors to poor health.

⊛ Do what you can to reduce stress in your life: Trim down your schedule; meet with friends for support; get professional help if difficult issues are pressing in on you; feed your spiritual life.

⊛ Include guilt-free relaxation in your daily routine.

4

Taking ✣ Control of ✣ Your ✣ Journey Through ✣ Menopause

I DON'T RECALL my mother ever mentioning the word *menopause*. Like most women of her generation, she didn't breathe any word even remotely related to human sexuality.

I had given the topic of menopause little to no consideration when frightening symptoms suddenly interrupted my life in my mid-forties. While visiting out-of-town relatives, I began hemorrhaging with an unmanageable flow that sent me to the nearest emergency clinic. I had never heard another woman talk about this scary occurrence, and I assumed I was seriously ill. The doctor at the clinic was kind and helpful, assuring me that what I was experiencing was normal—for a woman my age.

"What do you mean?" I asked.

"You're a little young for menopause to begin, but not unusually so."

"Menopause!" I couldn't believe it. I was nowhere near fifty, what I believed was the appropriate age for the onset of menopause. How could something this embarrassing be "normal"? Nothing I experienced that day felt normal to me.

The doctor gave me a shot of estrogen and prescribed birth control pills for five days. He advised me to see my doctor for tests to rule out anything serious and to decide on treatment.

Anything serious?! Treatment!

My life took a dramatic turn that day. What began as one incident evolved into five years of disruption. Everything about menopause surprised me. I had no idea of what to expect.

But there is no reason for you to have the same experience. Today books on menopause fill the shelves of most bookstores. The burgeoning ranks of baby-boomer women are well into this midlife season, and, fortunately, they're talking.

One reason there is so much discussion about menopause is the debate swirling around the traditional treatment of the day for the problems that may occur during menopause and the regimens often prescribed to prevent subsequent health problems. Since its introduction in the 1930s, hormone replacement therapy (HRT) has been controversial. Confident claims of symptom relief and protection from osteoporosis and heart disease are tainted by suspicion that HRT increases the risk of breast cancer.

The latest reports chronicle the drug industry's attempts to find a safe remedy to offer its growing market, but opinions about the best treatment conflict, even within the medical community. Some studies show little risk of breast cancer, while others suggest the risk is a valid concern.

One could spend years evaluating whether to choose this treatment or another. What's a woman to do?

I've made some suggestions in the following pages, but you hold the most important piece of your menopause puzzle. You must choose treatment based on your health, symptoms, family history, and personal comfort level.

To encourage you, let me add that at fifty-two, I feel wonderful. I had a hysterectomy to stop the recurring hemorrhaging, and I no longer have menopausal symptoms that need treatment. Because I appear to be at low risk for heart disease (low blood pressure, great cholesterol level, weight within the desired range) and for osteoporosis (medium frame, dark complexion), I have chosen not to take HRT.

New information on this topic is being published every day. Paying attention to the latest research will help you make informed decisions that are right for you.

I was having lunch with a friend
I hadn't seen for a few years.
The conversation turned to health issues,
and my friend told me of her ongoing struggle
with a poor memory and hot flashes.
I was overjoyed!
Not at the news of her discomfort
but at the realization that much of what I felt
was normal.

❖

If you haven't talked to other women
who have experienced menopause,
you may feel alone and abnormal.
Talk to your peers.

When I did give thought to menopause,
I assumed it would be no big deal.
After all, it's a normal and inevitable stage of life
that all women go through.
Yet when it came, I struggled
with symptoms and decisions
I had never anticipated.

⚜

Just because something is normal doesn't mean
it will be easy.
Don't beat yourself up if you think you should be
handling this "normal" life passage
with more ease than you are mustering
at the moment.

It seemed like all of a sudden
I couldn't remember anything.
My doctor told me that memory loss
was typical for women my age.

⇜✧⇝

Men my age tell me they suffer from memory loss too.
Not ALL midlife maladies
are due to menopause.
Relax and become a good reminder-note writer.

I was an emotional wreck,
pacing and feeling anxious.
This was not my usual behavior.
I stopped and sat down to pray.
It didn't help.
I pulled out my Bible and turned to Psalms.
The words fell flat on my spirit.
I got up and got busy.
No good.
The anxiety passed in a few hours
but not because of anything I did.
I had other anxiety attacks,
but they were few and far between.
When they came,
I learned to ride them out and not panic.

⋆⋇⋆

Emotional ups and downs are
often a part of menopause.
Your usual coping mechanisms may fail you.
But know this: You aren't losing your mind.
Physiological changes are influencing your emotions.
Continue your research, and think about
how you want to treat this symptom.

I hate it when men tell jokes
about menopausal women.
I want to deck them—which would just reinforce
the stereotype they have of midlife women!

People often joke about things that
make them feel uncomfortable.
Be forgiving.
Most men don't have enough good information
to help them understand
this complex subject.

Be kind and compassionate
to one another, forgiving
each other, just as in Christ
God forgave you.

EPHESIANS 4:32

I sat in my doctor's office
discussing my upcoming hysterectomy.
"After the operation, we'll get you right on estrogen,"
           he said automatically.
"No," I politely interrupted.
"Remember, I don't want to take estrogen."
He shook his head, indicating his disapproval.
I didn't like disagreeing with an "authority,"
but I felt certain this was the right decision for me.

⚶⚶

Many doctors think estrogen is
the best treatment for all women
and will advise you to take it.
Carefully consider what your doctor suggests,
but remember that the decision is yours.

We met on a monthly basis for about a year:
seven midlife women talking about menopause.
We called ourselves the MSG.
Some people thought we were fond of spicy Asian food.
We knew it meant
Menopause Support Group.
And supportive it was.

Little else comforts like the company of those
who are facing the same dilemma we are.
Join or start a menopausal support group.
Just meet and talk, clip articles for all to read,
compare notes, laugh, and pray
together.

Two are better than one,
because they have a good
return for their work:

If one falls down, his
friend can help him up.

ECCLESIASTES 4:9-10

Sara was distraught.
She had been strengthened by her
faith in every previous trial she had faced.
Now at midlife, she found that her efforts
to go calmly through menopause
were thwarted by her fluctuating emotions.
She felt undone
and feared that God was
displeased with her.
Sara's menopausal symptoms were normal,
but she blamed them on her perceived
spiritual inadequacy.

~✦~

Your relationship with God isn't measured
by how you feel.
He is with you and loves you just as you are.
Believe that, even when you feel shaky.

As I was with Moses,
so I will be with you;
I will never leave you
nor forsake you.

JOSHUA 1:5

When I first read that menopausal symptoms can last for years,
I felt hopeless.
At the time it seemed that menopause
would never end.
Now those difficult days are
in the past.

⨳

Peri-menopause,
the technical term for
the symptomatic years leading up to
a woman's last period, ENDS.
It will be over.
Don't lose hope.

There is a time for everything,
and a season for every activity under heaven.

ECCLESIASTES 3:1

Recently I was talking with
a group of young women.
In the course of general chatter,
one of the women was lamenting about
missing an opportunity to go boating with some friends.
She went on to explain, in whispered tones,
that no bathroom facilities were available
for the day's excursion
and she was in the middle of a heavy period.

❧❀❧

It has been over four years now since I have had to consider
the inconveniences of monthly periods.
Menopause means freedom!

ADDITIONAL ÷ PRACTICAL ÷ HELPS

🕮 If you don't have a regular physician, ask friends for recommendations.

🕮 Schedule a doctor's appointment to have a midlife evaluation or to talk about symptoms you may be having.

🕮 Ask for a blood workup that will include measuring your estrogen levels.

🕮 If a doctor suggests you are at risk for osteoporosis, ask for a bone density test.

🕮 Check with your insurance company to determine which tests will be covered by your policy.

🕮 Be open with the doctor, and feel free to question his/her suggestions.

🕮 Check out the latest information on the topic. Visit your local bookstore, peruse current women's magazines, surf the Web.

🕮 Doctors often prescribe hormones and/or antidepressants for relief of anxiety. These may prove helpful for you, but be proactive in asking questions about the risks and side effects of these drugs and their full impact on your overall health.

🕮 Many women find that adjusting their schedule to include restful time for themselves helps with anxiety. Healthy eating and exercise also provide relief.

🕮 Reevaluate your commitments. If you are stressed and overloaded, simplify your life.

Enjoying * All * the Phases * of * Motherhood

GOD PLACES HIGH VALUE on motherhood. He even included the honoring of mothers in the Ten Commandments: "Honor your father and your mother, as the LORD your God has commanded you" (Deuteronomy 5:16). But by midlife most women are on their way to releasing their children from their primary care. It's a challenging transition.

My mother moved through this time with seeming ease. Somehow she figured out how to be a wonderful mother of a young child, a young woman, and then a midlife woman—all without causing me to feel she was intruding on my independence.

When I went off to college, I knew exactly how my mother felt about life and the best way to live it. Phone calls from her were not infiltrated with guilt-ridden messages about my inattention to letter writing. Neither did she burden me with repeated warnings about the perils of college life. Mom let go of me and took responsibility for her own sense of significance.

Even when I had my own children, my mother respected my

role as mother while offering her genuine love and concern for her grandchildren. Oh, she let me know when she thought I was messing up—like not dressing my infant warmly enough.

I remember taking Lisa to the doctor for her one-month-old checkup. I had her decked out in yellow sweater and knit bonnet in the middle of July. Lisa's delicate skin was prickly red, and her head was sweaty as I removed her little crocheted cap.

"Why do you have her so bundled up in this heat?" the doctor asked.

"My mother said that babies should be protected from drafts."

The doctor informed me that I should dress Lisa the same way I would dress myself. If I'd be too warm in a sweater and hat, then Lisa probably would be too.

I told my mother what the doctor had said, but she was unimpressed. She didn't badger me; she just shook her head when she saw my bare-headed babies. My mother expressed her opinion, but she deferred to my judgment.

I've tried to do that with my own children. (What they don't know is how much I don't say!) I'm trying to respect them as adults. And there is much to respect. Both are loving and responsible young women, gifted in many ways and exemplary mothers to their young children. But they are still my girls. I struggle with reining in my protective instincts and allowing them to live life on their own.

It's a challenge to shift from being a mother of children to being a mother of adults. This adjustment was long and arduous for me. I loved mothering, even when my daughters were teens. I am still most content when we are all under one roof. I relish the dinners or holidays when my girls and their families are right here at home with Steve and me.

Not all women feel this way. Many are ready to enjoy the empty nest and easily let go as their children reach adulthood. For them, the changes are just as significant, but they may adjust more quickly.

Today some women also decide to start or continue their families much later in life. These mothers face the challenges of midlife while handling the exhausting—though rewarding—task of rearing young children. Midlife mothers of young children need to consider their own limitations when they are tempted to compare themselves to younger women with little ones. The parenting style they adopt may include more personal time and more attention to their own well-being than that of younger mothers.

Midlife also confronts the woman who has never had a child with the reality that she never will. At least she will not give birth to biological children. Depending on her expectations and desires, this can be a difficult time.

These scenarios mean we need to reframe the way we think about ourselves. If you have never had a child but want one, what options do you have? Is motherhood a realistic dream or one that you need to surrender? If you have children, you may need to let them go and open yourself up to the fresh opportunities this new stage of life brings. Your children will always be your children, but how you relate to them will change.

Mothering adult children is all about adjustment. Strong feelings of love, protection, and concern live on, but the way we express them needs to be adapted to the changes in our children's lives.

The day I left my oldest
child at her college dorm,
I was crying,
and she was too.
I don't know how long she cried,
but I cried for days.
I thought my heart would break.

Even good changes
can be painful.
Enjoy them,
and weep at the same time.

The righteous cry out,
and the Lord hears them;
he delivers them
from all their troubles.

PSALM 34:17

My daughters are both married now.
Their old rooms are still
full of teddy bears and
high-school memorabilia.
I asked them if they wanted
to take some of these
things to their own homes.
They both said no.

While they want their independence,
many adult children like
to preserve their presence
in the home of their youth.
If possible, allow for that.
It eases the separation and continues
to demonstrate
your love for them.
They don't outgrow the need
to come home to Mom.

I sat in the gym today with my grandson Alex on my lap.
He was busy chewing on my finger in an attempt
to force his first tooth through his gums.
As I held my grandson, I watched his mother and his aunt
fill the roles of coach and assistant coach
for the girls' junior varsity volleyball team.
It seemed like only yesterday that I sat in the same gym
and watched my daughters play on the teams they now instruct.
The day seems far away when I may be cheering for
the little one now cutting teeth.
I'll bet the time will fly.

Enjoy your children today.
Don't wish them older sooner.
That day will come quickly enough.

I ran into Cathy at the grocery store.
She looked down in the mouth
and greeted me unenthusiastically.
When I asked her what was wrong,
she told me she didn't know what to do with herself.
Her youngest had gone off to college a few months before,
and the time Cathy had looked forward to for years
was proving to be empty.
We talked about the
feelings of insignificance
that creep in after so many years of active mothering.

Mothering is a full-time endeavor.
When our children are grown,
we may flounder a bit before discovering
new ways to find meaning and purpose.
Give yourself time.

God could not be everywhere
and therefore he made mothers.

JEWISH PROVERB

"I think my kids are too focused on money
and worldly success," a friend told me recently.
She went on to say she was going to
call her son and remind him of what is important.
She asked me if I thought she should.
I said, "No."

＊✦＊

When you've advised or commanded someone
for almost twenty years,
it's hard to hold your tongue.
But wait before speaking to your adult children.
They probably know how you feel
without you saying a word.
In general, give advice only when asked—
or when you are so burdened
that you can't *not* speak.
Then gently express yourself
and free your children
to do what they will with your input.

"I'm acting just like you, Mom,"
Lisa said to me.

PREFERENCE

"There's a radio station that plays
music from the '80s all day Saturday.
I love to turn up the volume
and hear it all over the house."
My daughter was referring to my preference
for "golden oldie" stations that play
music from the '60s.

IMPRINTS

＊＊＊

Your children carry imprints
that reflect who you are.
Enjoy the comfort of knowing that
parts of you live on in them.

LIVE ON

Molly hung up the phone and wept.
Her daughter had called to say
her marriage was over
and divorce was imminent.

We wish our children could learn life's lessons
without going through pain.
Hug them, weep with them, pray for them.

*I long to put the experience of fifty
years at once into your young lives,
to give you at once the key to that
treasure chamber every gem of which
has cost me tears and struggles
and prayers, but you must work
for these inward treasures yourself.*

HARRIET BEECHER STOWE
letter to her twin daughters

I went to my daughter's house to pick up my grandson.
As she was getting dressed to go out, Lisa started screaming.
In the next twenty-four hours she suffered a miscarriage.
The pain of watching my child suffer so profoundly
was almost paralyzing.

～✤～

For some reason we think that if we can just
"get them raised,"
the painful part of mothering will be over.
But love doesn't grow up and disappear.
It just gets deeper and deeper.

Lisa, Lara, my friend Susan, and I
went away for the weekend.
Alex came too because he was only
two months old.
Susan has no children of her own
but has been active in the lives of my girls
for almost twenty years.
I watched my daughters laugh and talk with her.
While we were shopping, they would point out jewelry
and pull clothes from racks and pronounce,
"Suz, this looks just like you!"
She would hug them and love on them,
as if they were her own daughters.
She is a blessing in their lives.

⋆⟡⋆

Women who have no biological children
are not limited in the love and care they can offer to others.
Welcome them into your life.
Give generously of yourself.

The other day I went to a girlfriend's house for coffee.
I took my two-year-old grandson along.
My friend's three-year-old daughter was a perfect playmate.
There we were, close in age ourselves,
watching my grandchild and her child play together.

Sometimes in midlife, women find themselves
mothers again.
Take time to adjust to surprises—
and enjoy.

Joanie is a forty-six-year-old mother of two boys,
ages six and three.
Most nights she falls asleep exhausted.
While she loves her sons, Joanie says that
becoming a mother late in life has not been easy.
"I could keep up with them a lot better
if I were in my twenties," she told me.
Still, she would not have it any other way.

Life is full of trade-offs.
Young mothers sometimes wish they had
the greater freedom and flexibility
their childless days afforded.
Midlife mothers often wish they had more energy.
But women who decide that mothering is
part of God's plan for them
find that his help—and that of others—
gets them through the tough years.
Hang in there.

Restore to me the joy
of your salvation and
grant me a willing spirit,
to sustain me.

PSALM 51:12

6

Welcoming ∗ the
Changing ∗ Seasons
of ∗ Marriage

TOM AND CAROLYN were both forty-eight years old when their youngest child graduated from high school and moved into his own apartment. After spending twenty-four years rearing three children, this couple was looking forward to being a twosome again.

"We were married right out of college and had our first baby within two years," Carolyn said. "I was ready to do some things for myself that I'd put off for years, and I was ready to be alone with Tom."

While Carolyn's daily routine changed dramatically with the departure of her youngest child, Tom's didn't change at all. He got up, left for work, and returned home at six o'clock, just as he always had. "The first few weeks were great," he said. "I'd get home, and Carolyn was excited about her day, energetic, talkative.

Then something happened. She seemed anxious, unsettled. When I'd ask her what was wrong, she'd seem mad at me. It was a confusing time."

Tom and Carolyn found themselves in the strange transition between parenthood and "couplehood." "We hadn't really talked about what it would be like," Carolyn mused. "Oh, we'd daydreamed about having more freedom and less responsibility. But we hadn't realized that our day-to-day life would be so affected. I was definitely more surprised than Tom was, probably because my whole framework of how I functioned had changed. I loved the freedom, but I hadn't figured out what to do with myself. Tom still had the structure of his work, and I resented that his life seemed so undisturbed.

"We realized that we needed to talk, to decide how we wanted to live now that the kids were grown. We needed to look at the way we related to each other and to talk about ourselves as people, not just as parents."

Many couples with children find themselves at the same crossroads as Tom and Carolyn by the time they reach their fifties. For many years their relationship has been lived out in the context of being parents. Left alone with each other, they discover they need to redefine, reevaluate, and reaffirm who they are as husband and wife during this next phase of their lives.

When a couple has no children, these same needs appear but more gradually. There isn't a specific day when the structure of their relationship is altered, but sometime in their forties or fifties, they realize their lives are half over. The pressure of diminishing time raises questions about the quality of their relationship.

This season in a marriage can be exciting and invigorating. It can breathe life into the mundane and stir the spirits of partners whose relationship has been forged through years of togetherness. As midlife impacts your marriage, being aware of the most common transitional issues will help you shift gears and welcome the future.

The lighted candles cast a warm glow
throughout the restaurant.
Soft music and whispered conversations
complemented the romantic ambiance.
Jim and Kathryn had planned this special occasion
to mark their reemergence
into life as a twosome.
They studied the menu, ordered with delight,
and smiled at each other over crystal goblets.
Neither could think of anything to say.
They had nothing to talk about.
Nothing.

❧

Years of busyness—even good busyness—
may render a relationship speechless.
Recognize the need to talk,
to verbalize how you feel.
Talk about yourself, your partner,
your dreams, hopes, fears.
Encourage the same vulnerability
from your spouse.
Now is the time
to start talking AND listening.

Mary sat with head in hands
as the unpaid bills lay before her
on the kitchen table.
Ed's company was downsizing,
and his manager had told Ed he had to go.
Close to retirement age, they hadn't
anticipated beginning again.
But begin again they did.

Sometimes we find our lives far different at midlife
than we had anticipated they would be.
Face and accept disappointments,
and reaffirm your mutual commitment to each other.

There is no more lovely, friendly
and charming relationship,
communion or company
than a good marriage.

MARTIN LUTHER

I cleaned out some bureau drawers the other day.
It must have been quite awhile
since I had done such a full sweep through my belongings
because I found lots of buried treasure, long forgotten.
Under the cotton and flannel, I discovered
silk and lace delicacies I hadn't worn in years.
How humiliating.
I had extended my desire for comfort
into all areas of my wardrobe.
The good news was that I didn't have to
go out and buy anything.
Lovely goodies lay at my fingertips.

＊＊＊

Romance may have slipped away in the midst of familiarity,
but it can bloom again.
Rummage through your closets and drawers for
        forgotten enticements.
If you don't find any, head for the mall.
Seduce your husband.
It's okay with God.

I am my lover's and
my lover is mine.
SONG OF SONGS 6:3

DIFFERENCES

When I married Steve,
I thought I could convert him into an extrovert.
I also thought I could instill at least a moderate interest
         in classy clothes.
But my husband prefers to huddle at home in
         his flannel shirts,   ACCEPTANCE
which he enjoyed long before they became a fashion staple.
Now I find myself choosing the home fires
more frequently than the social scene.
The classy clothes—that's another issue.
I continue to cultivate an interest in style.
Steve gives me articles on fashion
from the numerous newspapers he peruses.
We accept and celebrate
         each other's differences.

Acceptance of each other at midlife is freeing.
You are free to change or to remain as you are.
Your spouse may not have turned out as you expected.
You didn't either.   UNIQUENESS
Celebrate each other's uniqueness.

EARLY RETIREMENT

Larry was a Los Angeles policeman.
Nina worked for Los Angeles County.
They took early retirement and moved to Colorado.
He loved woodworking, and she loved interior design.
They now have their own business,
with Larry as the craftsman
and Nina as the design and finishing expert.

DREAMS

Partnering in vocations or avocations
can bring new purpose and energy to your midlife years.
Talk with your spouse about your dreams
for fulfillment in the future.
Even if restraints or responsibilities prohibit
a complete change of direction,
you can explore how to incorporate what you love
into ventures—or adventures—in your marriage.

CHANGING DIRECTION

Monte and Linda love to spend
quiet evenings together reading.
After their boys were grown and out of the house,
this couple converted a small, upstairs room
into a reading nook.
They fashioned it after a Swiss chalet
with wood paneling and paintings
collected during their travels.
Two rocking recliners
and tables stacked high with books
take up most of the space in their hideaway.
They relish the peaceful aloneness—together.

⚜

Years bring a comfortable peacefulness to a relationship.
Enjoy each other in ways that nurture both your souls.
You don't have to use a lot of financial resources to do this;
you just have to think creatively.
Ask God to open your minds
to the possibilities.

Ask and it will be given to you;
seek and you will find;
knock and the door will be opened to you.
MATTHEW 7:7

Years ago my daughters and I
took my parents away for the weekend.
We met friends of my parents at a big band dance
held at the Ice Arena in Vail, Colorado.
The ice had been covered with a wooden floor,
and tables were set up around the dance area.
Charlie, my father's college classmate,
had been in a wheelchair for years.
His wife, Jean, a feisty, petite woman,
buzzed happily around Charlie and tended to his every need.
As the band played, Charlie's and Jean's smiles at each other
were evidence of their fond memories.
Then, as the chords of "Let Me Call You Sweetheart"
filled the arena,
Jean stood up and put her arms around Charlie.
She sweetly lifted him to his feet.
He held her in a waltz embrace
as they swayed slightly to the music.
His feet, unable to move, were anchored to the floor,
but clearly his spirit soared.
Tears poured out of Jean's closed eyes
as she silently mouthed the words to the old, familiar song.
My daughters and I watched with our own smiles and tears.

Aging doesn't rob us of experiencing some of the
sweet moments of youth.
Continue to build new memories
and enjoy the ones formed years ago.
Enjoy the memory—and reality—of
your lives and love together.

Love is patient, love is kind.
It does not envy, it does not boast, it is not proud.
It is not rude, it is not self-seeking,
it is not easily angered, it keeps no record of wrongs.
Love does not delight in evil but rejoices with the truth.
It always protects, always trusts, always hopes, always perseveres.
Love never fails.

1 CORINTHIANS 13:4-8

Sometimes when I get busy,
I let the laundry pile up.
If he needs socks or something,
Steve will do a few loads himself.
He doesn't sort clothes the way I would.
And he lays some things to dry on the bed
instead of on a rack I use for just that purpose.
I get annoyed.
Then I stop and think and feel petty for being irritated.
Steve doesn't bug me to do the laundry;
he does it himself, without complaint.
And that's not all.
He vacuums, cleans up the kitchen,
takes care of the houseplants,
and handles all manner of fix-up jobs.
What's a little difference in the way we do laundry?

Midlife can bring perspective.
Most things are not worth fighting over.
We are better able to shrug off minor differences
when we see them in light of the goodness
of the whole relationship.
Ask yourself if any given argument is worth continuing.
If it is, communicate with care.
If not, kiss and make up.

"Every Friday, we have a video date-night," Mary told me.
She and her husband of almost thirty years
have raised three children
and now enjoy many simple pleasures
that were crowded out during the busy parenting years.
"We go to the video store, then pick up Chinese take-out food.
Then we come home and relax in the comfort and quiet
of our own home.
We don't answer the phone,
and sometimes we watch two videos,
staying up into the late hours of the night.
We love having the time to just enjoy each other."

❧❀☙

Midlife often means we've reached an age
when we have the flexibility to do things
we've let go for years.
Revisit your dreams of peaceful enjoyment,
and make plans.

After Lara left for college,
I would wander into her old room
and linger.
Steve would find me
lost in thoughts and memories
and ask what I was thinking.
He would listen to my ramblings
about missing her and being glad she was doing well.
Then he'd listen to me express my disbelief
that her sister was about to be married.
"How can I be old enough to have children this old?" I'd ask.
He'd give me a hug
and tell me he loved me.

A marriage relationship can be a stabilizing constant
in the midst of midlife changes.
Tell your husband how glad you are
that he's with you.

7

Appreciating
Your ❖ Sexuality

WHEN MY LITERARY AGENT suggested I include sexuality as a topic in this book, I grimaced.

"Lois, you need to do this," she pressed.

"I don't want to," I whined.

She didn't need to ask why I was hesitating. She knew, as most
of us do, that sexuality is one of those dicey subjects that hits us at
the core of our vulnerability: *What will happen to me when I am
no longer attractive, desirable, sexy?*

In our sex-crazed culture, it's possible to forget that our
sexuality—our femaleness—involves much more than how appeal-
ing we are to members of the opposite sex. Our sexuality is an
integral part of how God made us. It includes the totality of who
we are as women, with all the characteristics that make us different from men. We reveal our femininity in all our interactions, not
just in the specific acts of sexual expression.

But when we reach midlife and experience the physical changes
it brings, we may feel threatened as we relate intimately to our

husbands. *Will he still find me as attractive as he once did?* And the single woman who hopes to marry may struggle to feel hopeful in the midst of what seems to be diminishing appeal. *What man would want me now?*

No amount of cosmetic surgery, makeup, or youthful clothing can mask the outer manifestations of physiological changes inside our bodies. With age comes the loss of vitality. Put bluntly, we dry up. Some of us dry up only physically; others also experience parched libidos. The pulsing hormones that birth sexual desire have ceased to flow. In their place can be an emptiness or numbness that can result in disinterest in making love.

Emotionally, sexuality is about being wanted. Aging supposedly robs women of those enticements that create desire in spouses and admiration in casual observers. We stand stripped and afraid that we no longer have the allure to keep the love of the man in our life or capture the love of one yet to arrive. No wonder we don't want to talk about sexuality.

If it were true that aging brings an end to sexuality, we'd be singing dirges about the demise of our essential femaleness. We'd slump into the categories labeled "dull," "drab," "dry," "old maid," "hag," "toothless crone," and on down into the dark hole of horrifying images. If sexuality had only to do with looks and sexual performance, we might find ourselves banished to some neutered never-never land, never to feel desire or desirable again. But the truth is, we are born and live and die as sexual beings. God created us as male and female. Our sexuality is good, and it is permanent. Despite threatening changes, sexuality does not have to wither with age.

As I pointed out earlier, many of our images of ourselves as older women were cast when we were teenage girls. From that pinnacle of desirability, we looked at older women with disinterest or pity. We seldom thought about how our own desirability would change as we aged. Perhaps we need to rethink our definition of sexuality and exchange our youthful images for ones of women who are whole beings. A woman who has matured in her understanding of sexuality knows she can express it by her acceptance of herself, her confidence in the love and care she brings to relationships, and her appreciation of God's creative design, which assures her of lifelong feminine identity.

It's true that how we express our sexuality may change. We may not have the desire or ability to make love as long or as often. Our bodies may have lost their firmness or be scarred by childbirth or surgery. But it's also true that we can be captivatingly feminine women at any age. We may never grace the cover of a magazine or model a bikini, but we can be comfortable with ourselves and enjoy the confidence that brings.

What's more attractive than that?

The three of us decided to splurge
and go to the Ritz Carlton for lunch.
Claudette, Janie, and I settled at our table by the window,
looking out on the pool and ocean.
As I surveyed the menu,
my eyes kept lifting over the top of it,
drawn to a buxom blond and her adoring beau
who were dining poolside right outside our window.
Our table fell unusually quiet as all three of us
caught ourselves staring at the young woman
in the low-cut halter top.
Her body was flawless, her figure the very image of sexiness:
full breasts, tiny waist, slim hips, long legs.
We glanced at each other and started to laugh.
Here we were, three middle-aged women
gawking at the cultural ideal of feminine sexuality.
We made a few jokes about the demise of our own desirability,
sighed, and turned our talk to the comfort of good food
and good friendships.

Who among us hasn't bought into
our culture's image of desirable sexuality?
Understand that other images do exist and are attainable.
Be willing to change your thinking.

I, like most American women,
receive a plethora of mail-order catalogs.
Beautiful, young, curvaceous women adorn the pages
of many of these advertising enticements,
but none more so than *Victoria's Secret*.
I used to pore over each page of this company's
sumptuous and frequently printed catalog.
A few years ago I realized that I was
comparing myself to the catalog's models
and feeling bad about myself.
Few of us could order the wares these size-six women display
and not be disappointed by the reflection
we see in our mirrors.
While I still find the clothing desirable,
I have chosen to look at it in a store,
draped over a hanger,
instead of clinging revealingly to a perfect body.

It's hard not to buy into society's ideal image of sexuality
when it is ever before us.
Throw out those catalogs BEFORE you look at them.

I was in the mall the other day,
walking behind a woman with cascading black hair.
Her tight skirt was very short,
and the heels on her shoes were very high.
We both entered a department store
and headed in the same direction.
She suddenly turned around and walked back past me.
I was surprised to see the face of a woman
well over fifty.

Our attempts to maintain youthful sexuality by
dressing like young women
just make us look foolish.
Give up revealing clothes and girlish hairstyles.
No need to look frumpy.
Become comfortable with yourself and then
dress in ways that express that comfort.

"I have no interest in sex,"
a midlife female friend said to me.
Once she began peri-menopause,
her libido disappeared along with her waist.
Her experience is not uncommon; it's just seldom talked about
by women in their midlife years.

❧

Your desire for sexual intercourse may lessen.
If you are married, talk openly and honestly with your spouse.
Often libido returns, not so much
as a result of physiological changes
but because emotional confidence
and a supportive partner's love
infuse the mind and heart with passion.
Sexual love can then move to a deeper level.

Patty and Mike are in their early fifties and enjoy
a fulfilling sex life. Patty admits that her desire did wane in her
mid-forties, but she and Mike talked about how she felt.
He was a patient and understanding listener.
He told Patty he still loved her and found her as
desirable as ever. He was complimentary and affectionate,
without being demanding.
Patty's appreciation for Mike and her love for him
ignited a fresh desire toward him.
While she no longer feels the rush that hormones can give,
she does enjoy the physical expression
of sexual love that they share.

When we pay special attention to the marriage relationship,
desire can be rekindled.
It usually isn't the same as the hormonally-driven desire of youth,
but one enlivened by true intimacy.
It begins not in the biological systems of the body,
but in the mind.
Growing young in our attitudes and perspectives
stirs passions that reside deep within the soul.
Nurture your relationship with your spouse:
Spend time alone together, talk, listen,
express care and affection.
And be patient.

I was speaking on the topic of menopause
at a women's conference.
Afterward, a woman stopped to talk to me,
but she waited until everyone else
was out of hearing range.
She softly and timidly told me that she
no longer felt sexually attractive because
intercourse was so uncomfortable and
sometimes even painful.
We talked about the embarrassment associated
with the onset of vaginal dryness.
She told me she felt like an old, wrinkled crone.
I understood.

❈

Physical changes, like vaginal dryness,
can be helped with medications.
More and more over-the-counter lubricants
are appearing on the grocery market shelves
near the feminine hygiene products.
Check them out and talk with your doctor.

I used to engage in disparaging rhetoric about myself.
I think I was attempting to explain the obvious:
I'm getting older.
Steve hated it when I did this.
So we talked about my feelings
and the realities of aging for women.
He assured me that I was, and am,
attractive and desirable,
but I would still blurt out the negatives
I was carrying around in my own mind.
Finally he realized that his assurances
made little difference.
I needed to change my thinking.
As long as I clung to the myth that
sexual attractiveness belongs only to the young,
I was doomed.

✨

Midlife sexuality is about change.
We cannot continue to equate our
desirability with physical attributes.
Read, reflect, talk, reflect, pray, reflect.
Let God change your mind about
what is sexually attractive.

> Do not conform any longer
> to the pattern of this world,
> but be transformed by the
> renewing of your mind.
> ROMANS 12:2

When we had a baby shower at our house
for my daughter Lara, a good friend of mine
came whom I hadn't seen for about a year.
Throughout the evening, I noticed the younger
women being drawn to Colleen.
She did look wonderful, but it was her manner,
her attitude, her sense of fun that held her audience.
As everyone was getting ready to leave,
Colleen began to tap dance with one of our young guests.
She and eight-year-old Lindsay were shuffling on my
hardwood floor while others watched and applauded.
Colleen admitted she felt great about herself and
had even resumed the tap-dancing lessons
she'd given up years ago.
I asked her if the class was for women our age,
and she assured me that she was
the grandmother of the bunch.

Midlife sexuality is about confidence.
When we feel good about ourselves, it shows.
Thank God for who you are
and risk learning more about yourself.
It could be fun!

Mandy had been married for twenty-five years.
She still was talking about every little thing
that displeased her about her husband.
Midlife didn't seem to be bringing them closer together.
She moved, and I didn't see her for several years.
When we met again, I couldn't believe the change.
She looked refreshed and peaceful,
and she spoke lovingly about her husband.
When I asked her what had happened,
she said that she had finally looked inside herself
and faced her own demons.
She spent some time in counseling
and got serious about her relationship with God.
The external transformation was startling.

Midlife sexuality is about congruity.
When we are content and fulfilled internally,
it shows on the outside.
Honestly analyze what eats you up inside.
Get help, if you need to, and move toward being content
that the internal you complements the reflection in the mirror.

8

Making * the * Most
of * Singleness

I WAS MARRIED THE FIRST TIME when I was not quite twenty-one. Jack was the big man on campus in high school, and I thought I was the luckiest girl in the world when he started dating me after we graduated.

By the end of our junior year in college, we decided to marry. I walked down the church aisle on the arm of my father, certain that the young man beaming at me from the front of the church would be in my life forever. We would grow old together and die in each other's arms.

It didn't happen that way.

After just thirteen years of marriage, my young hero was killed in an accident. We were both thirty-four when he went to heaven, and I became single again.

When we marry, none of us anticipates that we will be widowed until, perhaps, we're very old. All of life is ahead of us. And I have never spoken to a divorced woman who suspected that the relationship she planned to enjoy for life would end bitterly. We all make our marriage commitment with the intention of honoring it. Despite this, divorce happens, even for Christian couples.

One of the factors affecting marriages during midlife is the often-referred-to male midlife crisis. A man who experiences this stereotypical phenomenon reaches his forties or fifties and realizes his youth is slipping away. He experiences many of the same emotions middle-aged women feel and turns to the admiration of a younger woman to boost his ego. His wife, struggling with her own feelings of inadequacy, has her worst fears confirmed: she isn't attractive enough to hold her husband's interest. Instead of being supported and understood during midlife, she finds herself deserted by the one she wants to trust the most.

Divorce at any age is complex and results from multiple factors. But the scenario of a man deserting his middle-aged wife for a younger woman symbolizes the plight that so often accompanies aging: We feel like we become less. Less attractive, less desirable, less important. This isn't true, but such beliefs can be a powerful influence on an unstable marriage. Instead of partners redefining their relationship and appreciating each other's finest qualities, they give up and look elsewhere.

Whether single through divorce, death, or never being married, being single and middle-aged can be challenging. For many it is lonely and lonely and lonely.

I didn't remarry until I was forty-four. By that time I thought I might never remarry. The statistics grow increasingly grim for women as they age. The numbers of available men decline, while the ranks of single women swell. Just check out any singles groups. The older the participants, the fewer the number of men.

But we are not statistics. We are beloved children of a loving heavenly Father, and he can change our life circumstances in a moment. Of course he may choose to allow us to live single for the rest of our lives, or we may choose singleness ourselves. Whatever the circumstances may be, the single, middle-aged woman can experience fulfillment and joy.

When Elaine was diagnosed with cancer,
her husband of twenty years said that
he couldn't take the stress of her illness.
He left her.

✢

The peace of God can
infiltrate the painful places and
soothe the piercing agony.
Understand that peace and pain
can coexist.

The Lord is close to the
brokenhearted
and saves those who are
crushed in spirit.

PSALM 34:18

Eileen's husband left
after twenty-five years of marriage.
"My kids are grown, my ex-husband has a new wife,
and here I am," Eileen lamented.
"The other day my pastor told me he was praying
that I would meet a man soon
so I could go on with my life.
I walked away determined to begin
to get a life of my own."

Often the church doesn't know
what to do with single women—
or with anyone who is going through a major change
that stirs up profound emotions, doubts, and questions.
But God does.
Talk to him, be honest,
and ask him to show you how to embrace
the next stage of your journey.

Diane has been divorced for five years.
She was treated badly and suffered greatly.
When she called recently about getting together,
I found myself dreading being with her.
She still continually bemoans her loss.
I feel sad for her,
but I no longer want to contribute to her victim mentality
by listening to the same tragic story over and over again.
When confronted, Diane simply says that
no one understands how bad her life is.

Remaining a victim will rob you of joy.
After a time of healing,
partner with God to live again.
Let go of the past,
and don't dwell on
what might have been.

A friend called late at night.
Her daughter had decided to move in with her father,
my friend's ex-husband.
I felt powerless to help her.
All I could do was pray in the dark.

Prayer changes things.
Divorced people may not be reunited in marriage,
but God's love still touches them.
Pray for the reality of his love in your life
and in the lives of others.

And I pray that you, being rooted
and established in love, may have power,
together with all the saints, to grasp how wide
and long and high and deep is the
love of Christ, and to know this love
that surpasses knowledge.

EPHESIANS 3:17-19

The years between my first and second marriages
were full of blind dates that friends arranged.
Before each one I felt like a schoolgirl
getting ready for the prom.
I was excited and had great expectations.

～✦～

Divorce or death of a spouse at midlife often leads
to dating again.
You may FEEL sixteen,
but as an adult woman you will find that
your relationships are much more complex now.
Proceed with caution.

"He has no faults," I beamed as I told my friend
about my first dating relationship after being widowed.
But after a year of disappointments with him, I realized
that I was waiting for unfulfilled hopes to come to fruition.
I kept thinking about the "potential" of our relationship—
the way a young woman in love for the first time
sometimes naively accepts disappointments
in hopes of future change.

Our expectations for new relationships
are often based on potential, not reality.
Realize that at this age what you see is what you get.
We are all much more set in our ways
than we were when we were
young and in love.
Of course we can adapt and grow in relationships.
But basing our reality on potential
is risky business.
Be wise.

One night after I had been widowed for about three months,
I rolled over in bed and touched what I thought was an arm.
In the darkness of sleep,
I settled with my hand resting comfortably on Jack.
Jack's dead!
I bolted upright and saw the spare pillow next to me.
The moonlight spilled through the window
and illuminated my loneliness.

⤖✦⤖

I am often asked what the toughest thing is
about being widowed.
Loneliness.
Nothing takes it away.
So embrace it.
Don't fill up on busyness.
In time you will adjust to the separation
and the bearing of it will be easier.

Jackie and Ted had been
married for twenty years.
Then one day he dropped dead
on the golf course.
Weeks later Jackie finally emptied suitcases
she'd been packing the day he died.
They were to go on their first real vacation alone
in two decades.

＊＊＊

Just when you're free to enjoy life in new ways,
you lose your partner.
Grieve your loss.
Know that God will give you hope
and new plans.

"For I know the plans I have for you," declares the Lord,
"plans to prosper you and not to harm you,
   plans to give you hope and a future."

JEREMIAH 29:11

I was out of town and alone.
As I waited in line at the entrance to the hotel restaurant,
I felt anxious and uncomfortable.
It seemed that all eyes were on me,
wondering what I was doing there by myself.
I couldn't remember a time in my life
when I'd eaten alone in a public place.
Now hunger drove me to disregard my awkwardness
and sit at a table for one.
It wasn't so bad.
Over the years I've come to actually enjoy dining solo.

As you heal, you will get stronger.
You will become more at ease in situations
that feel strange.
Begin to take small risks and
move out in new ways.

"My kids think I'm crazy," a divorced friend told me.
"They don't understand why I'm quitting my job
and going to this training conference to prepare for a new one."
But Connie was excited about her newfound confidence
to make decisions that proved surprising to her family.
"I've thought about it, prayed, talked with others.
Now I'm going for it."
Connie's adult children shook their heads
and hugged this mother they hardly recognized.

❧❖❦

Half your life may well be ahead of you.
Be open to change.
Believe that God will direct you
in ways you never anticipated.

SINGLE

Tricia recently turned fifty.
She told me she still hopes to marry one day
but is no longer counting on it.
Single all her life, Tricia now more intentionally
focuses on the present and on enjoying the
mature perspective and the many good friends
that age brings.

MATURE

⚜

Never marrying doesn't mean that life
has passed you by.
The richness of friendship, the joys of life experiences,
the discovery of self,
and God's transforming power to shape
you into a woman after his own heart
are all within your grasp.
Enjoy today!

DISCOVERY

RICHNESS

"I never even thought about having children
until it was too late,"
Nancy said as she cuddled her niece's newborn.
Nancy had intentionally chosen
a full-time career and singleness,
planning to marry later in life.
Now, at age fifty-two, she found herself
alone with no children.
She admitted some regret.

We can't go back and rewrite our past.
Allow yourself time to think, reflect, and grieve.
Recognize the valuable impact you can
have on the children who are in your life.

Grandmothering
with ✦ Joy

I REMEMBER HER HANDS: cool and soft, even after half a lifetime as a farmer's daughter and a farmer's wife. Her bulging veins and the deep wrinkle lines that crossed her broad palms revealed the hard work of many years. But what I remember most of all is running my fingers across the back of my grandmother's hands and pinching the pliant skin between my fingers. When I let go, the puckered skin stayed puckered. Grandma would let me sit in her lap and play with her hands for hours while she read to me or told me stories.

Now my grandchildren sit on my lap and finger the loose flesh on the back of my hands. They pull and pinch and mold the skin as if they are playing with Silly Putty. They snuggle against me and let me nuzzle the tops of their heads while turning pages of storybooks I once read to their mothers. The delicious fragrance of baby skin and freshly washed toddler hair gives me more pleasure than the smell of bread baking in the oven.

My hands hold my grandchildren and love on them as much as

they will allow. And instead of feeling old, I feel connected. I remember the love I received and gave long ago, and I enjoy that same exchange two and three generations later.

Those not of this "club" might consider me...well, deluded. We've all been subjected to the sappy rhetoric of grandmothers as they gush about their offspring's offspring. We smile and nod indulgently as they display the plastic-encased string of pictures they carry in their purses. All the babies look the same to us, but we ooh and ahh and act like we, too, marvel at the uniqueness of each cherub. Then we walk away and wonder what happens to reasonable and intelligent women when they become grandmothers.

Well, I don't know that I will live long enough to explain what does happen, but it has happened to me. For certain. I am in love, filled up to overflowing, and eager to splash my euphoria onto anyone who comes within range. I display pictures of my grandchildren in every room of my house; I carry them with me in my wallet, planner, and suitcases when I travel. I bore friends with reenactments of conversations with my oldest grandson, who at almost four truly IS brilliant.

I know that I do it, and you know what? I'm glad. Because that's what grandmothers do. We love fully and unconditionally and enjoy our freedom from the responsibility of being the primary caregiver and disciplinarian. Grandmothers enjoy a position of privilege and honor. Our children appreciate our help—most of the time—and our grandchildren adore us.

There are exceptions, of course. Distance can limit our visits with our grandchildren, and poor family relationships can drag unpleasant consequences into the next generation. I feel great sadness when I think of women whose bond with their grandchildren has suffered because of strained relationships with children and other family members. I'm sure that no such situation has an easy fix, but working hard toward a solution would be well worth the effort.

For most women, grandmothering is one of the purest joys of the midlife years and beyond. It is, indeed, all that it's cracked up to be.

The phone rang at 5:00 a.m.

I grabbed it, knowing something must be wrong.

Lisa's panicked voice told me that she and Chadd were
on their way to the emergency room with Justin.

His fever had reached 103 degrees, and
he had been screaming most of the night.

I jumped out of bed, threw on some clothes,
and was out the door within minutes.

As I entered the emergency room,
I saw Lisa walking back and forth trying to soothe her son.

As I walked up to them, I felt the tears in my eyes.

"Nana," Justin cried softly, with arms outstretched.

As I took him from Lisa I could smell the fever.

He clung to me, and I began to walk with him.

Lisa collapsed in a chair, her head in her hands.

"Thanks, Mom," she whispered.

❧

Giving comfort to a grandchild is doubly rewarding.

You help your children while helping theirs.

Don't underestimate even the small things that you do.

Her children arise and call her blessed.

PROVERBS 31:28

Lisa and Justin and I were out shopping one day
and ran into a friend of hers I had never met before.
When introduced, the friend said that
I didn't look like a grandmother.
Before I could thank her, Lisa chimed in,
"Yes, she does!"
I started to protest, then realized that
Lisa also meant her comment to be a compliment.
I know she thinks I look good,
but she wants me to be her children's grandmother
and to be recognized as such.
It is the highest compliment she can give.

Being a grandmother means you have
the opportunity to occupy a place of
high regard with your children.
Enjoy being called what you are: Grandmother.

Children's children are a crown to the aged.
PROVERBS 17:6

We would sit together for hours,
my grandmother and I.
She'd read to me or
play board games or dolls.
Sometimes we'd cook something fun, like cookies,
or we'd go for a walk.
She had time for me.

The quality AND the quantity of time
you spend with your grandchildren matter.
If distance separates you, become a letter writer
as well as a phone connector.
Give of yourself and your time as generously
as you can.

> I will very gladly spend for you everything
> I have and expend myself as well.
>
> 2 CORINTHIANS 12:15

The note on the front door read,
"Come on in, Lois—baby sleeping."
I slowly opened the door and tiptoed
into Judy's family room.
She was sitting in her recliner
with her granddaughter fast asleep in her lap.
I sighed and she sighed,
and we smiled with the knowledge
that only two grandmothers
can share.

⚜

Holding a sleeping child-of-your-child
floods a grandmother's soul
with peace and contentment.
Praise God for his unspeakable goodness
in the giving of little ones for us to relish—
even more thoroughly the second time around.

I was babysitting Alex,
who at six months of age
loved to sit in his saucer
(the current version of a baby walker)
and be entertained.
I found myself performing high school cheers for him.
I was jumping and motioning and sis-boom-bahing
as he watched and laughed out loud.
Later it occurred to me that
anyone else watching
would have thought me the fool.

❧✤☙

Grandmothers are allowed
to revisit youth.
Act like a fool with your grandchildren.

The great thing about getting older is that
you don't lose all the other ages you've been.
MADELEINE L'ENGLE

Justin and I go to the famous five-star Broadmoor Hotel
several times a month when the weather is fair.
We cut through the opulent hotel lobby, ride up the escalator,
and head out to the walkway around the lake.
We go over the bridge and head for our island—
a small patch of ground at the far end of the lake.
It isn't ours exclusively, but we pretend it is.
Our island is overgrown with foliage, and little inlets provide
resting places for the resident ducks to huddle in.
We examine crawling things on our hands and knees
and sit very still so birds will stop and sing near us.
Sometimes we are explorers, and other times we are hunters.
(I don't like to be a hunter, but Justin does.)
We take sticks and poke around in the dirt to see what lives
beneath the soil. We laugh and whisper and get dirty
and have a great time.

Young children can bring us back
to the wonder of God's creation
that is right in our own backyard.
Go on an adventure with your grandchildren.

> From the lips of children and infants
> you have ordained praise.
>
> PSALM 8:2

I sometimes visit an aerobics class at a nearby health club.
Whenever I'm there, I see one particular woman
who appears to be a regular.
She's in great shape, as evidenced by her energetic workout
that lasts the full hour at high intensity.
One day I heard her talking to another woman
about her grandchildren.
I smiled to myself.

✦

The mold for the stereotypical
grandmother has been broken.
Be yourself.

The other day Lisa asked me to tell her the story
about when I fell through the ice on a pond
when I was a girl.
"What made you think of that?" I asked.
"Justin was telling it—his version—and when
I asked him where he heard it,
he told me his Nana told him."
"Mom," she went on, "he loves for you to
tell him stories
that he can then retell himself."

❧

Our experiences enrich
the lives of our grandchildren.
Share your memories
with this eager young audience.

After I was certain Alex was asleep,
I tiptoed into his room.
His steady breathing assured me that
my presence hadn't disturbed him.
I gently placed my hands over his back,
touching him ever so lightly.
The silent prayers I'd offered up over the years
for my children and my other grandson
now went heavenward for this new baby.
I could almost hear the rustle of angel wings
as other guardians hovered by his crib.

❧✦❧

There is power in our prayers.
Pray diligently on behalf of these little ones.

I walked into church and saw Elizabeth
patting a baby cuddled against her shoulder.
She was walking in the back of the sanctuary,
cooing to the fussy child.
Within minutes his little head dropped in sleep
and all was quiet.
I didn't know whose baby it was,
but I was certain that some young and weary mother
was enjoying a break as this midlife saint cared for her child.
Elizabeth has no children of her own
but is often seen lovingly holding and rocking and snuggling
the little ones of others.

Biology isn't all that makes a grandmother.
Whether or not you have grandchildren of your own,
reach out with a loving touch to any children around you.
You will be a blessing.

Caring ✤ for ✤ Your Aging ✤ Parents

WHEN I WAS TWENTY-ONE YEARS OLD, I made my first visit to a nursing home. My husband's grandmother was placed there after breaking her hip and losing her mobility. I remember the smell more vividly than anything else. The pungent odor of urine seeped through the Clorox fumes that attempted to mask the unpleasantness.

Grandma sat in a wheelchair gazing off into an invisible world of her own. The scent of mothballs clung to her faded bathrobe. The mustiness of unwashed hair filled my nostrils as I bent to hug her.

Her three roommates were in similar states of disconnectedness and disrepair. They didn't seem to notice when Jack and I spoke to them.

A nurse came in with a tray of miniature fluted pastry cups that held each patient's prescribed medication. She perfunctorily passed out pills of varying shapes and colors, waiting to make sure her charges actually swallowed these life-preserving remedies.

Grandma didn't respond when we talked to her. She nodded

and patted Jack on the hand, then she silently drifted back into another world.

Our stay was brief, our exit hasty. Once in the car, Jack and I both professed that we would never let one of our parents end up in a place like that.

Most of us who are now in our forties and fifties have similar recollections associated with the perils of old age. And most of us have uttered promises to ourselves or to our parents that we would do everything possible to spare them such an end. During midlife many of us will be faced with determining just what God would have us do to honor our aging father and mother. Many of these decisions will be prompted by our parents' declining health.

Because my mother died suddenly at home, I never had to consider how best to care for her once she couldn't care for herself. But that was not the case with my father. He had always been a tough man, both in temperament and in physical constitution. Aside from a profound hearing loss that could not be overcome by the use of a hearing aid, he was in good health until his mid-eighties.

Then suddenly he suffered from severe dementia. One day his memory was fine. The next day he couldn't remember much of the previous forty-or-so years. He was hospitalized in the psychiatric ward of a local hospital for evaluation. I spent my days at the hospital and my nights trying to grasp what had happened to my once strong father. He had turned from a stubborn, independent old codger (by his own admission) into a docile, confused, and needy octogenarian.

My father was hospitalized on a Tuesday, and on Thursday of that same week, I was told I needed to find an appropriate place for him to live by the following Monday. I was shocked! Find a place for my ailing father to live in only four days?

That began for me a season that is both sad and stressful for many at midlife. We are faced with parenting our parents and admitting our own limitations in being able to care for them. Those who raised us are now completely dependent on us for their well-being. It's like having young children, very *big* children. Protecting—or even reasoning with—aging parents can be difficult. They aren't pliant and teachable but set in their ways. Even in the best scenarios, our parents can wear us out. It's a tough process to witness and to endure.

I did find a place for my father but not on the first try. His mind was a jumbled mass of conflicting thoughts and emotions, but his legs worked just fine. After he slipped out the door of the dementia wing several times, the nursing home staff told me that they could not keep him.

I started calling other nursing homes and care centers listed in the phone book. Either they had no spaces available or they lacked the proper facilities for my father's condition. Finally, one nurse told me about a home about forty miles away that was designed just for dementia patients. The whole facility was fenced in so the patients could roam freely inside and on the grounds. I made an appointment for that afternoon and headed out of town.

The first whiff upon entering the nursing home brought back memories of long ago. It was spanking clean, but the distinctive odors that seem to be linked with the elderly just can't be masked. The director showed me around, and I began to breathe again. The patients seemed free, yet they were closely monitored. They moved from hallway to lounge to yard and back to their rooms as they wished. The staff was friendly and kind, willingly answering my every question.

My father spent the last three years of his life with those specially gifted caregivers. Once he was settled in his room, I no longer worried about his care. Sadness always tagged along with me when I visited him because he was not the man I had known for the first forty-seven years of my life, but I no longer looked at nursing homes with one broad, condemning glance. I thanked God that some facilities existed where the staff really cared about the patients and could meet their specific needs.

Fortunately, not all of our parents spend their final years in nursing homes. Some are mentally and physically active right up to the end. Others slow down but don't require hospitalization or special care. In all cases, however, we become aware that those who raised us are near the end of their lives this side of heaven. There will be a parting.

A few years ago, Nancy Reagan addressed the Republican National Convention and referred to her time with her husband as the "long goodbye." President Ronald Reagan suffers from Alzheimer's and is slowly slipping away from the woman he loves.

I think Nancy Reagan's words accurately describe what we all face as our parents age. It is a bittersweet time filled with challenges, memories, and day after day of letting go. Our parents are leaving us, often slowly, and we are called to endure the long goodbye.

When I was looking for a place for my father to live,
I visited many nursing homes.
As soon as I left each one,
I went to a restroom and washed my hands.
So many people were drooling.
Then I felt guilty.

NURSING HOMES

One of the most painful aspects of watching parents age
is knowing how humiliated they would be
if they could see themselves as others see them.
Change the lens through which you view old age.
Look right through the wrinkled skin
and past the loosened mouth
to see the heart of the one who raised you
and sacrificed for you in love.

SACRIFICED

When my father had eye surgery,
he needed drops in his eyes
three times a day.
I felt annoyed at the interruption
as I drove over to his house
to put the drops in.

～✦～

An African proverb describes children
as the walking stick for their aged parents.
American independence doesn't foster a glad willingness
to care for the old and infirm.
If a parent's health challenges irritate you,
pray that God will give you a spirit of gladness as you
fulfill your responsibilities.

Daddy and I were sitting in the lounge
at the nursing home.
A woman near us was leaning over and moving her arm
through the air as if she were stroking a dog or cat.
She spoke lovingly to the invisible pet
and patted it with weathered fingers.
"She's crazy, you know," my father said in all earnestness.
"Oh really?"
"Yeah." He smiled and leaned over to whisper to me,
"She thinks there's a dog there. Can you imagine?"
We laughed together.

My father seemed so lucid and coherent,
and yet he was part of the "crazy" woman's community.
In the middle of dismal situations, humor helps.
Infuse your tough times with laughter.

Humor

I cradled the phone between my ear and shoulder
as the 911 operator calmly led me through my
frantic attempts to save my mother's life. She struggled
to breathe for only a few brief moments.
Then she was still.
I put my mouth over hers and blew in.
I followed the instructions of the kind woman
on the other end of the line.
But I knew my mother was gone.
I felt strangely old and grown up.

The death of our parents removes the barriers
between us and our own mortality.
While I hadn't relied on my mother for advice
in years, I had always felt the comfort of her
presence, love, and concern.
When our parents die, we occupy
a new place in our family.
We become the matriarch and gain a greater
opportunity to impact those who follow us.
It is not a position of dominance but one of wisdom.

You never get over being a child,
long as you have a mother to go to.
SARAH ORNE JEWETT
The Country of the Pointed Firs

The day after my father died,
my daughters and my grandson went with me
to the nursing home to gather his belongings.
Before going to the funeral home to make arrangements,
we stopped at a playground near the nursing home.
Justin was happy to run around and make some noise,
and before I knew it, Lisa and Lara were swinging and laughing
and reminiscing about their childhoods.
As I watched the two generations after me,
I, too, remembered.
I remembered the sense of fun I'd learned from the man
whose belongings we'd just loaded into my car.
Part of him was still playing that day.

Some of our most treasured values come from our parents.
Notice them in your life
and in the lives of your children.

There are boxes of jewelry
tucked away in my closet.
Some of the contents have moved from storage
to my own jewelry box,
but a lot of it remains unworn since my mother died.
Sometimes my daughters and I pull out the boxes
and spread the jewelry all over the floor.
Memories flood in.
We may pick up a pin and decide to wear it,
or take a pair of clip-on earrings to convert to pierced ones.
I'm so glad I have these things my mother loved.

Your parents' treasures will become your own.
Don't get rid of their belongings too quickly.

I missed my father's last birthday.
Lisa and I were going to visit,
but we got busy.
Oh, that sounds so awful.
I regret not going.
He died a month later to the day.

✦

We will have regrets as our parents age
and as they leave this life.
Ask God's forgiveness for what you did
or didn't do—
and forgive yourself.

Some ÷ Practical ÷ Advice...

⊛ If your parents are still mentally competent, talk with them about their medical and financial plans and resources. These topics are difficult to broach, but they are easier to handle later if you know what your parents prefer. Find out if they have a current will, a living will, and preferences for care if they become mentally incompetent.

⊛ If your parents' health begins to deteriorate, ask them to consider when (and if) they would be willing to assign power of attorney to you or one of your siblings. This gives you the authority to make decisions for them in the event they are unable to do so. If your relationship is not one that will allow for this level of trust, try to resolve differences and begin to build that trust.

⊛ If your parents are willing and have not already done so, consult an attorney about the advisability of having your name added to your parents' legal documents, deeds, etc.

⊛ Many resources are available to help you determine how to best care for your aging parents, even when their mental capacities are limited. One of the best ways to find out what is available in your area is to talk with a physician who deals primarily with geriatric patients. This area of professional expertise should be listed in the Yellow Pages of your phone book.

⊛ Talk with others who are dealing with the same issues. Some of the best advice for choosing nursing homes, doctors, and treatments comes from people who have already had to cross these bridges.

Cherishing
Your ⚜ Friendships

SUSAN AND I ARE PLANNING a trip to Europe together. We're thinking about visiting France and Italy, places dripping with culture and ambiance.

It's been more than fifteen years since we traveled internationally together, and many things will be different. We won't be getting up at the crack of dawn to explore, and we won't be shopping till we drop. We won't consider our trip a failure if we don't stay up past midnight or see all the sights listed in Fodor's guidebook. For us, the exotic lives most vividly in our imagination. Our spirit of caprice is what sprinkles spice into our lives.

This excursion will provide a parenthesis in the lives of two midlescent women, allowing us to walk the streets of history together—ours and those of antiquity. We will talk, sit in sidewalk bistros sipping café au lait, people-watch, reminisce about days past, dream of days to come, and enjoy the goodness of seasoned friendship.

In midlife our friendships become more mellow and restful. We have learned what makes relationships mutually nurturing, and we gravitate toward women with whom we can establish or continue lasting friendships. We are less concerned with how many friends we have and more focused on the depth of the relationships we cherish.

We don't need to travel together in order to enjoy the rewards of each other's presence. We don't even have to live in the same city. Some of my best friends are miles away, but we are present with each other over the phone lines. We've laughed and cried together. We've prayed for each other. Our children have been blessed by the love and prayers that flow to them through these women who love us.

And now we can sit together and share our surprise that we're this age. These conversations with our peers temper our shock and soften the realities of growing older. We appreciate each other more with each passing day, grateful that the communing of souls sweetens all of life.

When I was in high school, my friends and I memorized
Vince Lombardi's famous speech on winning.
We were often heard to quote,
"Winning's not the most important thing, it's the only thing."
Competition was a vital part of life.

As we grow older, we develop
a deep appreciation of other women.
Competition is replaced by a spirited love for each other
and a willingness to share the laurels of life with our friends.
Praise others.

Colleen and I don't see each other often,
but when we do, it's always pleasant.
Now that our children are adults CHALLENGES
and have families and challenges of their own,
Colleen and I still have a lot to share.
So when she stopped by one day,
I eagerly brewed a pitcher of iced tea,
REMINISCE
and we sat down to sip and reminisce about times
when our children were in high school together.
We recalled the past with laughter and tears
and told new stories
with an appreciation enriched by our shared history.

⚜

Even if our paths don't cross often,
old friends can continue to touch our lives profoundly.
Stay in touch. TOUCH LIVES
Write that note.
Make that phone call.
Stop by and visit.

Claudette called the other day to tell me
that her mother had fallen and broken her hip.
And so begins my friend's complex task
of helping her mother make major life changes.
I can relate.
I helped my own mother through the painful loss of her leg
to the ravages of diabetes.
Claudette and I now talk almost daily across the miles.

Friends who have been through situations
similar to our own are a special comfort.
Rely on them to help you during times of stress.

No medicine is more valuable, none more
efficacious, none better suited to the cure of temporal
ills than a friend to whom we may turn for consolation
in time of trouble—and with whom we may share our
happiness in time of joy.

St. Aelred of Rievaulx

Carry each other's burdens, and in this way
you will fulfill the law of Christ.

Galatians 6:2

We talk for hours, my female friends and I.
Some of them know me so well, they see much in me
that I don't see.
They are an essential part of the way
God works in my life.

The maturity and wisdom of women
who have reached midlife
are profitable to us in many ways.
Take advantage of the counsel of your
mature friends.

As iron sharpens iron,
so one [woman] sharpens another.

PROVERBS 27:17

"I'm just so shocked,"
a friend said to me upon the news of her sudden job loss.
I sympathized with her apparent anxiety at
having to scurry around and get another job
after many years with the same company.
"I just never expected to be middle-aged, alone,
and unemployed all at once," she said.

Some of the changes at midlife are more
unexpected than others.
Job loss is one of them.
Call on encouraging friends who can help you walk
through the difficult process of finding new employment.

A friend just called to ask me to pray for her
husband, who is seriously ill.
My friend and I are close in age.
We've lived through many trials.
"You know how to pray," she said.
"Yes, I do. And I will," I replied.

When we've reached this age,
we can identify with so many of each other's challenges.
We do know how to pray.
Pray for one another.

The prayer of a righteous [woman] is
powerful and effective.

JAMES 5:16

One of my favorite ways to spend an afternoon
is to meet a girlfriend for coffee and conversation.
We talk of many things.
When we were young girls, we focused on boys.
When we were young women, we focused on boyfriends,
husbands-to-be, husbands, children, careers.
Now we are seasoned sisters.
Our conversations are spiced
by a variety of life experiences.

As we age, we bring to each other the gift of new learning
birthed from a wealth of living.
Meet and talk with your friends.
They'll enrich you.

Tammy and Irene had been friends for years.
When Irene's husband died suddenly at age fifty,
Tammy was there.
After a few months passed and other people had
gone back to the routine of their lives,
Tammy was still there for Irene.
She talked with her every day—and many nights.
She visited often
and invited Irene to remain closely connected with her family.
She talked and listened and prayed and helped Irene
learn to make a new life for herself.
Tammy was the person who made the biggest difference
in Irene's journey through many difficult years.

Friendship can be costly.
It can also be worth the price.
Be a good friend.

> A man of many companions may come to ruin,
> but there is a friend who sticks closer than a brother.
>
> PROVERBS 18:24

Resting ✤ in ✤ the
Promise ✤ of ✤ Immortality

I CANNOT THINK, SPEAK, OR WRITE about the frailty of life and finality of death without reference to the death of my first husband. *Reference...* As if his dying is now only a footnote to the present fullness of my life. It's not the truth. Daily I bear the imprint of that immense loss.

Death separates. The loss of our loved ones leaves us wandering, tripping over empty spaces and shrinking from the screaming silence that once was graced with the presence of someone now gone. Thoughts of our own mortality perch us on the brink of a mysterious passage that seems to present the ultimate threat: the ending of our very existence as we know it.

When thoughts of death creep in, we may dodge and evade these mental intruders while youth defies demise; but by our mid-forties or fifties, we begin to face our own mortality. Ernest Bramah, English short-story writer and novelist, said, "One cannot live forever by ignoring the price of coffins."

But those of us who know Jesus as Savior can transcend the

heartache of loss and the dread of death. We can bask in the eternal embrace of God's love, revealed most splendidly in the promise of our immortality. The dark passage is only a passage, not a destination. The angel of darkness is defeated by the royal Conqueror on his white horse (Revelation 6:2). Faith in Christ breathes eternal life into each of us who accepts him as Lord.

Sometimes, though, even for those of us who believe, heaven's promise of immortality seems ethereal and elusive. Our vision is blurred. We become shortsighted, stuck in the here and now. Understandably so.

My son-in-law, Chadd, is walking through the valley of loss as his father endures the painful end of his life this side of heaven. Chadd and two of his brothers spent a week with their parents as arrangements were made for hospice care during their dad's final weeks of battling cancer. The day after Chadd returned home, he came to our house to pick up his boys. As we sat and talked and cried, Justin climbed into his father's lap and cuddled close to him. Justin sat quietly, patting Chadd's chest with his little hand.

On the way home, Justin finally spoke from his four-year-old perspective.

"Dad, I don't want you to feel sad about Grandpa," he said.

"It's okay to be sad, honey," Chadd responded.

"I want to go see Grandpa."

"Well, we'll see. But you know, Grandpa is going to heaven soon."

Justin, knowing his Grandpa Jack had "gone to heaven" in a balloon accident, asked hopefully, "Is a hot-air balloon coming to get him?"

In the mind of a believing child, a vehicle of death was transformed into a transport to eternity.

By the time we reach midlife, our ability to see through the eyes of childlike faith is weakened. But fortunately for us, God's promise of immortality doesn't wane even if our hope falters. As we embrace the reality of our mortality as well as God's gift of immortality, we can wrestle with the pain of the one in light of the glory of the other.

In a recent three-month period,
I attended memorial services for four men.
I wept through all four services.
My tears were the evidence of mixed emotions:
sadness for the losses the families were suffering
and gratitude to God for his enormous gift
of eternal life.
I cannot hear a song or a sermon
or a word of any kind about heaven
without crying.
I am filled with awe at what lies ahead
for those of us who love God.

Heaven is a really big deal.
Thank God that this life is nothing close
to all there is.

No eye has seen,
no ear has heard,
no mind has conceived
what God has prepared for
those who love him.

1 CORINTHIANS 2:9

I sat by the bed of my friend as he lay close to death.
We spoke of heaven.
As I looked at him, I got excited in the midst of my sadness.
He was about to enter a perfect place
where he, and all who believe,
will live forever.

Look past this life into forever.
Develop an eternal perspective.

"Do not let your hearts be troubled. Trust in God;
trust also in me. In my Father's house are many rooms;
if it were not so, I would have told you. I am going
there to prepare a place for you."

JOHN 14:1-2

"Do you think Daddy can play basketball in heaven?"
Lara asked me several months after Jack died.
"Yes, I do," I replied with little worry about
the accuracy of my theology.
Whether heaven literally contains basketball courts or not,
I don't know.
But I do know that it will have all we need
to enjoy perfect peace forever.

⚜

Most of us have a very limited view of heaven.
Ask God to expand your vision
of what is to come.

Then I saw a new heaven and a new earth, for the first heaven
and the first earth had passed away, and there was no longer any sea.
I saw the Holy City, the new Jerusalem, coming down out of heaven
from God, prepared as a bride beautifully dressed for her husband.
And I heard a loud voice from the throne saying, "Now the dwelling of
God is with men, and he will live with them. They will be his people,
and God himself will be with them and be their God. He will wipe
every tear from their eyes. There will be no more death or mourning
or crying or pain, for the old order of things has passed away."

He who was seated on the throne said, "I am making everything new!"
REVELATION 21:1-5

Jim had cancer and had been given little hope
that he would live much longer.
He got up in front of the church congregation and
spoke of his faith, his doubt, and the amazing grace of God
that filled him with peace and praise,
even as he faced death.
A few months later, many of us who had heard Jim speak
sat at his memorial service.
Person after person got up
and talked about Jim's impact on his or her life.
He lived fully,
faced death with an honest mixture of fear and longing,
and left a legacy that showcased God's faithfulness.

When facing their darkest moments,
people of faith often demonstrate
God's grace in their lives.
Be encouraged by their victories.
There are victories ahead for you, too.

Death, the final curb on freedom,
has itself suffered a death blow
through the resurrection of Jesus.

MICHAEL GREEN
Jesus Spells Freedom

I hated going to an attorney AGAIN
about amending our wills.
Steve and I had been married a few years
but hadn't changed our wills to reflect our new lives.
It is rather unpleasant to so specifically address
what will happen when you die,
but taking responsibility now for those important decisions
will greatly help those you leave behind.

If you don't have a will, get one drawn up right away.
If you have one, revise it whenever your circumstances change.
Talk to an attorney to determine what the best
course of action is.

When Steve was doing research
for a book on Celtic spirituality,
we spent two weeks in Ireland.
Almost every day we found ourselves
walking through cemeteries
that held the remains of people who'd lived
hundreds of years ago.
Over almost every grave stood a cross—
a comforting symbol of victory,
reminding us that cemeteries are not where
the souls of the faithful reside.

Christ overcame death.
Rejoice!

Death has been swallowed up in victory.
Where, O death, is your victory?
Where, O death, is your sting?

1 CORINTHIANS 15:54-55

13

Savoring

Your ⚜ Yesterdays

M ANY WOMEN MY AGE enjoy conversations that are sprinkled with the phrase *Remember when...?* Remember when we wore loafers and bobby socks and long ponytails and evenly trimmed bangs? Remember when girls didn't call boys on the phone? Remember when we cried when our team lost the football game and leaped with excitement when our parents let us drive the family car?

Memories add color and texture to our past and dimension to our present. Our fond recollections can refresh our spirit and cause us to smile at the way we were.

I'm a card-carrying member of the I-Love-Nostalgia Club. Enamored with all things sappy, I often reminisce about the joys of yesterday. I reflect on those memories pleasant to recall and pass over scenes of painful times. I don't hide in my memories, but I do savor them, reflecting fondly on days gone by.

On our journey through midlife, nostalgia revives senses that were at fever pitch in our youth. We can feel young again and laugh and reminisce—and be grateful that while our youth may be fading, our ability to enjoy its memory is still very much alive.

God honors memory. In fact, remembering is a central theme of both the Old and New Testaments. The Bible is the recorded history of God's people, and through the stories of his faithfulness from generation to generation, we come to know God's character and his ways.

When we dip into our own memory banks, we frame and reframe our personal stories in ways that reveal God's work in our lives. Our unique history becomes part of our legacy, showcasing for future generations God's loving faithfulness.

Justin and I love to play airline pilot.
We make control panels out of cardboard boxes
and use an old atlas as our flight map.
Justin's the pilot, Captain Miller,
and I'm the copilot, Lieutenant Nana.
As we fly, I remember the fun of my own childhood,
when I loved to lose myself in play.

No matter how troubled the world becomes,
children can bring innocence and fun into our lives.
Remembering our carefree days of play
can give us hope for the present and the future.
Take a few moments to write a paragraph
describing a childhood game you used to play.
Share it with a friend or family member.
Smile at the past.

The other day I went through some of my father's papers
while cleaning out an old trunk.
I began to feel guilty about things left unsaid
and some of the difficult exchanges
we'd had over the years.

❧❀❧

Unpleasant memories can drag us down into
guilt, regret, and sadness.
Ask God's forgiveness for your past mistakes,
accept it,
and choose to think about more positive things.
Give up regret over things you cannot change.

Lisa, Lara, Justin, and I took a trip back east.
We went into my old high school,
a stately building with tall, white pillars across the entrance.
Inside is a large lobby that served
as the student gathering area
before classes, during breaks, and after school.
As we walked in, Justin, who was two years old at the time,
strutted his stuff as if he'd made a grand entrance there
many times before.
He swung his little arms, took big strides,
smiled and waved to a passing teacher.
Full of confidence and bravado, he was the miniature
image of his grandfather,
who'd strolled those halls with me
over thirty years before.
My young love and first husband was gone,
but here was evidence of his imprint,
living and breathing and acting
just like him.

CONTINUITY

Sometimes events in the present
propel us backward into memories of long ago.
When those moments come,
take comfort in the continuity of life.

On the same trip back east, we went to my
HANGOUT high school hangout,
The Charcoal Pit.
It was a restaurant that specialized in steak sandwiches,
        fries, and sundaes
named after the mascots of the local high schools.
Our mascot, called a dynamiter,
was a personified stick of dynamite.
As the girls and Justin and I drove to The Pit,
I rambled on about the glory days REVELING
when my friends and I packed the restaurant after
        basketball games,
reveling in the thrill of victory.
The Charcoal Pit was still in its old location,
but a lot had changed.
It was bigger, and the menu had expanded.
There were no crowds of kids.
I felt disappointed.
Then I saw that they still served a dynamiter sundae.
I chuckled and enjoyed the evening with my
RECREATE daughters and grandson.

＊

We can revisit places from our past,
but we can't recreate moments.
Go back, enjoy the memories, and make new ones.

When John F. Kennedy was assassinated,
I was sitting in a world history class.
A student interrupted the professor,
stood up in the auditorium
packed with over three hundred people,
and told us that the president had been shot and killed.
I remember every moment of that day.

Think about the historical events that have occurred
over the past thirty years of your life.
Many have been tumultuous and unsettling.
Thank God for his faithfulness to you
and to future generations.

Even though my grandmother died when I was only ten,
I remember her vividly.
My memories of her recall her laugh,
her gentle voice,
her tender care of me.
Her deep impact on my life lives on in recollections
that continue to warm my heart
over forty years later.

Love well, love often, love much.
Make memories for those you will leave behind.

To live in the hearts we leave
is not to die.
THOMAS CAMPBELL

Rediscovering ✦ God

B Y THE TIME I REACHED my mid-forties, I had been a
Christian for over thirty years. I'd been active in ministry for
almost half that time and considered myself to be decidedly evan-
gelical, conservative, and doctrinally settled. I had a cogent answer
for almost any question someone might pose about spiritual issues.

As I found myself swept into the midlife whirlwind, however,
some of my assumptions were challenged. My personal circumstances made me feel as if my life was out of control. My children
left, and my parents died. Hot flashes disrupted my days and nights.
My friends and I talked in hushed tones about our own mortality.
We reaffirmed our belief in God and his provision for us but won-
dered why we felt so fragmented.

We also began to voice questions we could no longer silence.
*If God brings peace, then why do I feel so bad? How can I have
real value apart from performing a job or being a good mother?
Why am I feeling invisible in my Christian community?*

We admitted feeling out of place. Church activities seemed to
focus on young families, and we were no longer a part of that
group. We wanted to serve, be mentors and role models, but we
felt inadequate to relate to the upcoming generation. Some of us had

more time to give to God and his people, but what should we do? Others were still working full time, some were consumed with caring for aging parents or raising grandchildren. We seemed to have more choices and less stability than ever before.

As I moved into my fifties, I stopped spouting easy answers to difficult questions: *What should we do about the poor? How should we impact culture? How should we treat believers whose opinions differ from ours?* I began to learn that the question *What should I do?* was the wrong one. My focus shifted to *Who would God have me be?*

Now I am discovering God in new ways. From the vantage point of midlife, I see that I have not arrived at some spiritual peak. Rather, I am still very much in the process of learning and growing. That's an exciting place to be.

A group of us was talking about midlife issues
when one woman timidly asked,
"Does anyone else wonder
if what we've been taught all these years is right?"
Her question was met with a resounding "yes!"
We discussed the value of rethinking what we believe.
Perhaps we held some of our convictions
only because other people had told us to have them.
As we evaluated our beliefs and values over the months ahead,
no one lost her faith
and no one ran away from God or his truth.
Being willing to ask hard questions of God
only strengthened our confidence in him.

❧

Midlife may bring questions to the surface
that you've ignored for years.
God can handle your doubts.
Ask away.

I accepted Jesus as my Savior
when I was a teenager.
I was so excited.
As the years passed, I learned more and more rules.
I learned how to pray
and how to have devotions
and how to study the Bible.
Unfortunately, my initial excitement was replaced with
"doing the right thing."

Having a relationship with God is not a thing we *do*.
It is a fluid, vital journey toward knowing and being known.
Take your relationship with God out of a well-defined box
and meet the living Being that he is.

As the deer pants for streams of water,
so my soul pants for you, O God.
My soul thirsts for God, for the living God.
When can I go and meet with God?

PSALM 42:1-2

When Jesus was asked a question,
he often answered by telling a story, a parable.
He didn't spell out answers;
he taught in pictures.

Each of our life portraits
contains evidence of God's presence.
Look closely for the brushstrokes of the divine.
You may be surprised by where they show up.

I used to compartmentalize my life.
Church was part of my spiritual life,
having friends over for dinner was part of my social life.
Now I see God in all of my life all of the time—
even when I'm just sharing dinner and laughter
with friends and neighbors.

※❖❖

Our relationship with God is not lived out in private.
We have the privilege of bringing him to others
in the simplest ways.
Welcome friends and neighbors into your life.
Draw closer to God together.

I was speaking to a group of women at a large conference
when one listener interrupted and asked me
a theological question.
I didn't know the answer and told her so.
On the speaker evaluation sheets,
many of the women wrote that they appreciated my admitting
that I didn't know the answer to a question.
They felt that people are often quick to give an answer
even when they don't understand the question!

Age brings a humble acceptance of our own ignorance.
Admit what you don't know,
and continue to learn.

Good and upright is the Lord;
therefore he instructs sinners in his ways.
He guides the humble in what is right
and teaches them his way.

PSALM 25:8-9

I once heard a wonderful man of God say that, when
thinking about the future,
we can turn the question marks in our minds
into exclamation points.
We don't have to know what's coming
but can trust that, with God,
we will not be alone
or without hope.

***

We don't have to know it all to be hopeful and at peace.
We know who is in control.

Sometimes I gain a new insight.

I read Scripture or pray or listen to a sermon or
    read something in a book.

A thought will hit me in a new way.

It's exciting.

But then I feel like I should call an authority

(whoever that might be)

and get permission to see a truth in a fresh way.

I resist making the call

and instead allow myself the God-given
    privilege of listening to his Spirit

as he whispers to my own.

I don't have to conform to any particular
    person's teaching;

I need only follow the solid truth of God's Word.

Relating to God more personally may result in
    new thoughts and beliefs

that others will disagree with.

Think carefully, pray fervently, listen to
    good counsel—

and rejoice that God speaks to you personally.

Enjoy the communication.

I have always been an extrovert.
I love being with others
and practicing my spirituality in an
outwardly expressive way.

EXPRESSIVE

But in the past few years,
I have been increasingly drawn to some
contemplative spiritual practices.
I find silence and meditation calming.
I enjoy reading the Bible

REFLECTION

and then spending time in quiet reflection.

✦

As we grow older, God often touches us in ways
we haven't experienced before.

TOUCHES

While we need to be aware of false prophets
and spurious teachings,
we can also free ourselves
to live outside some of the spiritual boxes
other people have constructed around us.
Never stop growing in your experience of God.

Growing ❖ Young

MY GRANDMOTHER LIVED with my family until her death at age seventy-eight. Her hopeful attitude about all of life infused my young spirit with strength. She was a woman of faith, and her faith only grew as she aged.

Grandma fed her soul with God's Word. I still have her Bible and the notes she wrote on now-yellowed snippets of paper. She didn't preach, but she lived so fully and peacefully that I knew she had an inner strength that gave her abiding hope. I never heard her complain, and I never heard her express fear about her future.

Her mind and her spirit sparkled right up to the end. Even in a day when aging wasn't a headline issue, she seemed determined to keep living and growing as long as God would allow. She accepted changes and limitations gracefully. She learned and laughed and grew and gave.

Because I have access to the same life-giving God my grandmother did, I have the same opportunity to move through midlife and beyond with joy. I hope that in some ways I will be like her. I hope I'll live fully until I take my last breath.

I believe that we become old only when we stop growing. Inner stagnation leads to death before dying. But if we continue to learn and grow, we are energized. We may not do cartwheels across our front lawns, but we can find joy in the present and look toward the future with hope.

When we "grow young," we become more accepting of God's wisdom and our own limitations. It becomes easier to let go of what we never could control anyway. Our concept of God gets bigger, and we grow more content. We find a freedom to be ourselves as God made us instead of focusing on who others want us to be. We continue to add to our wisdom by pursuing new endeavors, honoring our curiosity about God and his truth, and enjoying the wonder all around us.

Even as our bodies age, we can grow young in attitude and spirit. Hope invigorates us, and faith enlarges our vision of what lies ahead. Heaven becomes our destination. We embrace life while stretching our hearts toward eternity, where we will live in loving relationship with our Father forever.

About ⁘ the ⁘ Author

L OIS MOWDAY RABEY is a frequent seminar and conference speaker. Author of five books, she speaks on a number
of topics, including women of a generous spirit, living and leading
with integrity, the living side of loss, and the heart of a widow.

Lois also presents a seminar based on this book, *Growing
Young*.

For information, please contact:
Lara Van Hulzen
phone: (719)536-9741
fax: (719)488-2479